Everyday
Slow Cooker

Krysti's Delicious Chili,
page 120

Everyday Slow Cooker

260 recipes that practically cook themselves!

Oxmoor House®

Dear Friend,

When it comes to enjoying supper after a hectic day, there's nothing as satisfying, or as easy, as coming home to a meal that's waiting for you. And it's a breeze to do...simply pull out your slow cooker and select from these 260 tried & true dishes. From now on, suppertime will be a cinch! With just a few ingredients and these recipes, you can have a marvelous meal.

Get started by serving Maple Praline Chicken (page 42) or Mom's Fall-Apart Sunday Roast (page 58) for comfort food to please. Want sandwiches for supper? Try Heartland Barbecued Beef (page 150), Italian Meatball Subs (page 154) or Greek Chicken Pitas (page 165).

Need an irresistible side dish? Country Corn Pudding (page 179), Fettuccine Garden-Style (page 180) and Mac & Cheese (page 181) will become family favorites. Soups and stews simmer wonderfully in the slow cooker, but don't overlook the chance to "bake" a dessert in it as well. Satisfy your sweet tooth with Banana Pudding Cake (page 216), Triple Chocolate Cake (page 219) and Apple Pie (page 232). You'll find the perfect dessert for family get-togethers, a neighborhood potluck or just about any occasion.

Enjoy these recipes that are simple to prepare yet deliver on taste and presentation. There are also tips for using your slow cooker, so plug it in and get started. With so many delicious ideas to choose from, *Gooseberry Patch Everyday Slow Cooker* offers favorites for everyone.

Wishing you delicious dinners,

Jo Ann & Vickie
co-founders of Gooseberry Patch

contents

Company Beef
Bourguignonne, page 102

slow-cooker tips

The slow cooker is the essential appliance for all cooks who enjoy savoring the flavor of delicious dishes (and desserts, too) without spending countless hours in the kitchen. These tips make the cooking process even easier!

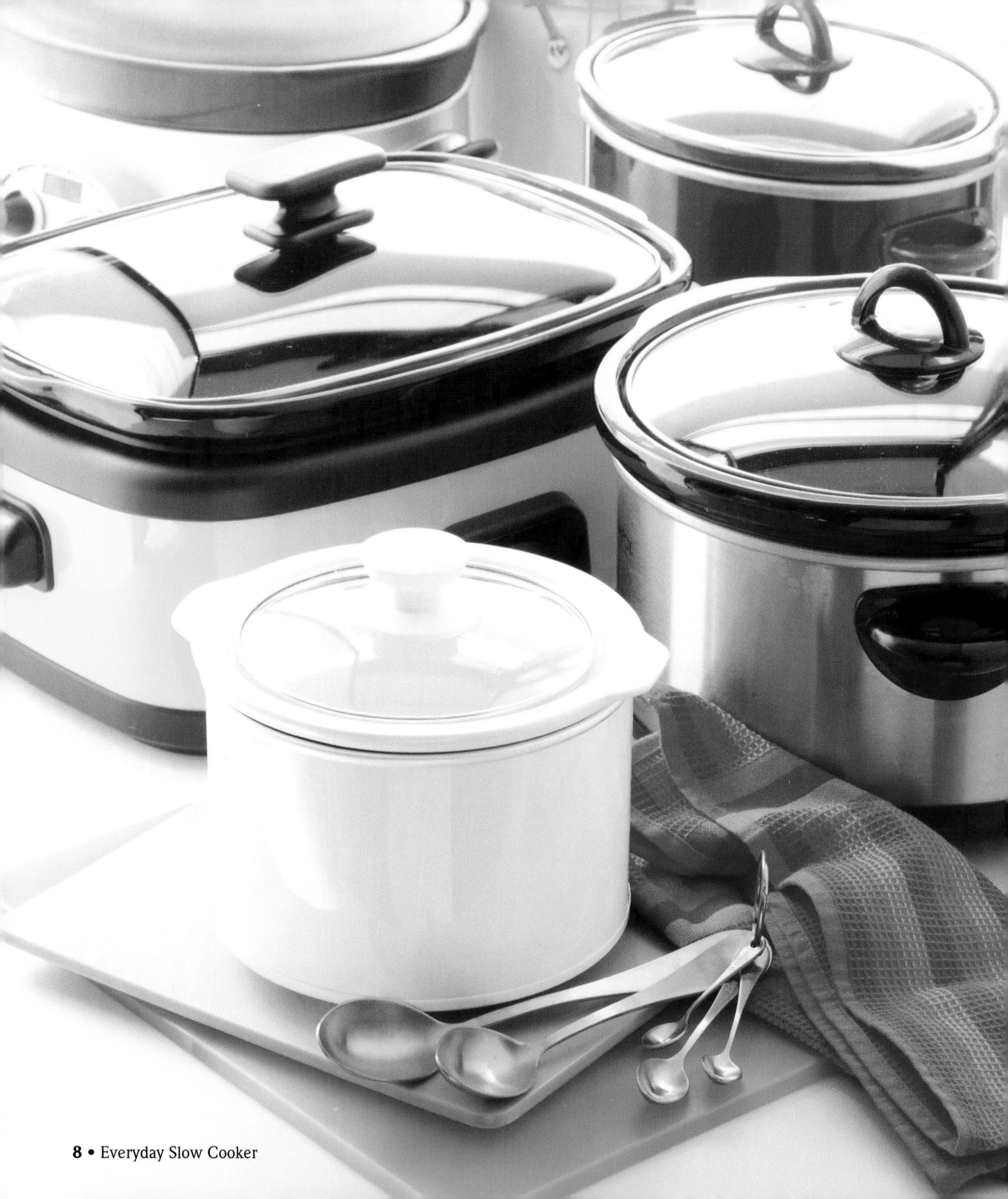

Shopping for a Slow Cooker

A slow cooker is a busy cook's best friend. After a hectic day at work or with appointments, there's nothing as satisfying as coming home to dinner that's simmered and ready to be enjoyed. There's little chance of overcooking the food if you follow these few tips, which will ensure a wholesome, delicious meal every time you use this convenient appliance. Plus, you'll find the clean-up is remarkably easy!

With so many slow cookers on the market, it's hard to know which one to buy. Here are some tips to help you get started.

Size matters. Consider how many you'll be cooking for when selecting a slow cooker. If you are cooking for yourself or a family of two, then a 3 to 4-quart size should work for you. Families of four or larger should look at a 5 or 6-quart slow cooker. Or, if you love to have leftovers or plan to use it for entertaining or taking to a potluck dinner, a 6-quart cooker is a good selection.

Removable inserts. A slow cooker with a removable insert is easier to clean than a one-piece unit. Depending on the manufacturer, the insert may be dishwasher safe. Some inserts can go from the freezer to the cooker, and some can even be used to brown meat on the cooktop before slow cooking.

Programmable timers. A programmable timer on a slow cooker is a nice feature if you will be gone all day. It allows you to set the cooking time; when that time expires, the timer will automatically switch the cooker to warm. If your slow cooker doesn't have one, purchase an external timer. Simply plug the external slow-cooker timer into the wall outlet, then plug the cooker into the timer.

quick clean-up

Follow these tips to make cleaning your slow cooker a little easier.

• The best time to clean the slow-cooker insert is shortly after taking the food out, while the slow cooker is still slightly warm but not hot.

• Even if you don't wash it at that time, rinse the cooker with warm water to prevent food from drying on it.

• Never immerse a slow-cooker unit in water. Simply unplug it, and wipe it clean with a cloth.

• To minimize clean-up, buy clear, heavy-duty plastic liners made to fit 3 to 6½-quart oval and round slow cookers. Place the plastic liner inside the slow cooker before adding the recipe ingredients.

• If you don't have slow-cooker liners, spraying the slow cooker with non-stick vegetable spray before placing the food inside will make clean-up much easier.

slow-cooker safety

Slow cooking is a safe method for preparing food if you follow the standard procedures.

• Fill your slow cooker at least half full but no more than two-thirds full. This helps meat products reach a safe internal temperature quickly and cook evenly.

• Defrost any frozen foods before cooking a dish that includes meat, poultry or seafood. This ensures that the contents of the insert reach a safe internal temperature quickly.

• Don't use your slow cooker to reheat leftovers because the cooker will not heat the food fast enough, resulting in an increased risk of bacterial contamination. Instead, use a microwave or cooktop.

Benefits of Slow Cooking

In addition to the convenience that allows you to make meals ahead, using a slow cooker offers these benefits:

• *Cleans up easily.* You have only one container to wash, or no container if you use heavy-duty plastic liners.

• *Environmentally friendly.* A slow cooker uses less electricity than the cooktop or oven. There's no extra heat escaping, so your kitchen stays cool.

• *Requires little attention.* You don't have to stand over a hot stove or watch the clock. The slow cooker works best when it's left alone to slowly simmer food. Generally, a little extra cooking won't ruin a dish.

• *Adaptable.* Most traditional recipes that call for long, slow, gentle cooking in a Dutch oven are adaptable to the slow cooker. Some of your family's favorite recipes can be ready as soon as you walk through the door at the end of a hectic day.

• *Economical.* Tough, less-expensive cuts of meat transform into tender, moist and richly flavored dishes when cooked in the slow cooker.

• *Healthier.* The tougher cuts of meat are also the leanest, and seldom do you add fat when cooking meat and poultry in the slow cooker. During the long simmering time, fat will rise to the top of the cooking liquid; remove it before serving.

• *Portable and versatile.* You can place the slow cooker anywhere there's an electrical outlet. It's especially useful when you entertain or when you have limited counter space. Prepare hot drinks and appetizers in the slow cooker and place the cooker where your guests will gather. Just make sure to use the low setting.

Slow-Cooking Tips

- *Leave the Lid On.* Don't lift the lid until the dish is done. The steam generated during slow cooking is part of the cooking medium. Opening the lid will release this steam and increase cooking time. It takes 20 to 30 minutes for the heat to build back up to the previous temperature after removing the lid.

- *Remember time conversions.* One hour on the high setting equals approximately 2 hours on low.

- *Cut uniform pieces.* When cutting meat or vegetables, be sure the pieces are the same size so they cook evenly.

- *Trim the fat.* Slow cooking requires little fat. Trim excess fat and skin from meats and poultry.

- *Limit the liquid.* You won't need much liquid; use only the amount of liquid specified in a recipe. Extra juices cook out of the ingredients, and less evaporation occurs than in traditional cooking methods.

- *Make-ahead option.* If your slow cooker has a removable insert, you can assemble the ingredients in the insert the night before for some recipes and then refrigerate the whole thing. Starting with cold ingredients may increase the cook time. If the insert is refrigerated ahead of time, don't preheat the base before adding the insert so as to prevent the cooker from cracking.

- *Add, don't stir.* There's no need to stir ingredients unless a recipe specifically calls for it. Simply layer the ingredients in the order given in the recipe.

- *Easy gravy.* You can thicken juices and make gravy by removing the lid and cooking on the high setting for the last 20 to 30 minutes of cooking time.

food tips

- Cut large pieces of meat in half before placing in the slow cooker to make sure they cook thoroughly.

- Veggies generally cook slower than meats. Place them under the meat in the slow cooker unless otherwise directed; direct contact with the bottom and sides of the cooker is helpful.

- Dairy and seafood tend to break down when cooked for an extended time. Unless otherwise directed, add milk and sour cream during the last 15 minutes of cooking and put in seafood within the last hour.

- Some of the new slow cookers cook at a slightly hotter temperature than older models. If using a newer model, check for doneness at the lower end of the range. If your cooker seems to boil contents, you may want to check for doneness a little early.

Spaghetti & Meatballs,
page 17

family-favorite main dishes

A slow cooker is a welcome friend, especially if you're a busy cook. Family-pleasing Poppy Seed Chicken, Beef Stroganoff or Chicken Cacciatore can be ready for the slow cooker in just minutes! Need a quick holiday meal? Turn to Easiest-Ever Turkey Dinner, giving you time to enjoy family & friends while the meal simmers.

Burgundy Meatloaf

A mixture of ground beef and ground pork can also be used.

2 lbs. ground beef
2 eggs
1 c. soft bread crumbs
1 onion, chopped
½ c. Burgundy wine or beef broth
½ c. fresh parsley, chopped
1 T. fresh basil, chopped
1½ t. salt
¼ t. pepper
5 slices bacon
1 bay leaf
8-oz. can tomato sauce

Combine ground beef, eggs, crumbs, onion, wine or broth, herbs and seasonings in a large bowl; mix well and set aside. Criss-cross 3 bacon slices on a 12-inch square of aluminum foil. Form meat mixture into a 6-inch round loaf on top of bacon. Cut remaining bacon slices in half; arrange on top of meatloaf. Place bay leaf on top. Lift meatloaf by aluminum foil into a slow cooker; cover and cook on high setting for one hour. Reduce heat to low setting and continue cooking, covered, for 4 more hours. Remove meatloaf from slow cooker by lifting foil. Place on a serving platter, discarding foil and bay leaf. Warm tomato sauce and spoon over sliced meatloaf. Serves 6 to 8.

Vickie
Gooseberry Patch

simple side

Create a fresh-tasting, crunchy salad your family will love! Simply toss together packaged coleslaw mix with add-ins such as raisins, dried cranberries or cheese crumbles and bottled salad dressing.

Best-Ever Lasagna
Cherylann Smith (Efland, NC)

This is a quick, easy recipe for homestyle lasagna. It's great with garlic bread and salad.

1 lb. ground beef, browned and drained
1 t. Italian seasoning
8 lasagna noodles, uncooked and broken into thirds
28-oz. jar spaghetti sauce
⅓ c. water
Optional: 4-oz. can sliced mushrooms, drained
15-oz. container ricotta cheese
8-oz. pkg. shredded mozzarella cheese

Combine ground beef and Italian seasoning in a bowl. Arrange half the lasagna noodles in a greased slow cooker. Spread half the ground beef mixture over noodles. Top with half of each of remaining ingredients. Repeat layering process. Cover and cook on low setting for 5 hours. Serves 10.

Pepperoni Pizza Rigatoni

Jo Ann (Gooseberry Patch)

Personalize the recipe by adding mushrooms, black olives or any of your family's other favorite pizza toppings.

1½ lbs. **ground beef**, browned and
    drained
8-oz. pkg. **rigatoni pasta**, cooked
16-oz. pkg. **shredded mozzarella**
    cheese

10¾-oz. can **cream of tomato soup**
2 14-oz. jars **pizza sauce**
8-oz. pkg. **sliced pepperoni**

Alternate layers of ground beef, cooked rigatoni, cheese, soup, sauce and pepperoni in a slow cooker. Cover and cook on low setting for 4 hours. Serves 6.

Mom's Cabbage Rolls

1½ lbs. ground beef
½ c. instant rice, uncooked
1 egg
1 t. garlic powder
½ t. salt
½ t. pepper
1 onion, diced
12 to 14 cabbage leaves

Mix together all ingredients except cabbage leaves in a large bowl; set aside. Drop cabbage leaves into boiling water for 3 to 4 minutes, until pliable; drain. Place ¼ cup ground beef mixture in the center of each leaf. Fold in sides, then roll to make a neat sausage-shaped package. Pour half the Sauce into a slow cooker; add cabbage rolls. Pour remaining Sauce over rolls. Cover and cook on high setting for 5 to 6 hours. Serves 4 to 6.

Sauce:

2 8-oz. cans tomato sauce
juice of 2 lemons
3 T. all-purpose flour
½ c. sugar

Combine all ingredients in a bowl; mix well.

Dixie Dill
Elkland, MO

"My mom gave me this recipe when I was a frazzled newlywed. It's simple and delicious, especially good on a cold winter day."

—Dixie

Spaghetti + Meatballs

This dish is perfect paired with a fresh green salad from your garden patch.

1 lb. frozen cooked meatballs, thawed
26-oz. jar spaghetti sauce
1 onion, chopped
1½ c. water
8-oz. pkg. spaghetti, uncooked and broken into 3-inch pieces
Garnish: grated Parmesan cheese

Combine meatballs, spaghetti sauce, onion and water in a slow cooker. Cover and cook on low setting for 6 to 8 hours. Stir well; add broken spaghetti. Increase heat to high setting; cover and cook one more hour, stirring once during cooking. Serve with Parmesan cheese. Serves 4 to 6.

Susie Backus
Delaware, OH

simple side

Garlic bread: Blend ½ c. softened butter, 1 T. chopped fresh parsley, 2 tsp. minced garlic and ¼ c. grated Parmesan cheese. Spread over Italian bread halves; broil 2 minutes.

Beef Stroganoff

A memorable meal doesn't require hours in the kitchen on your part...just a trusty slow cooker.

"A scrumptious dinner that cooks all by itself while you tend to the household, shop or just take it easy!"

—Jacque

1¾ lbs. boneless beef round steak, cubed
1 T. canola oil
½ c. red wine or beef broth
2 T. all-purpose flour
½ t. garlic powder
½ t. pepper
¼ t. paprika
¼ t. dried oregano
¼ t. dried thyme
¼ t. dried basil

10¾-oz. can cream of mushroom soup
0.9-oz. pkg. onion-mushroom soup mix
8-oz. pkg. sliced mushrooms
½ c. sour cream
8-oz. pkg. wide egg noodles, cooked
2 tablespoons butter, softened
Garnish: fresh parsley, minced

Brown beef in one tablespoon oil in a Dutch oven over medium-high heat 8 to 10 minutes. Add wine or broth to pan, stirring to loosen particles from bottom of pan. Combine flour and seasonings in a slow cooker. Place browned beef and mixture from pan on top; toss to coat. Add mushroom soup and soup mix; stir until blended. Stir in mushrooms. Cover and cook on low setting for 6 to 7 hours or on high setting for 3 to 3½ hours, until beef is tender. Stir in sour cream; cover and cook until thoroughly heated. Serve over noodles tossed with butter; sprinkle with parsley. Serves 6.

Jacque Zehner
Modesto, CA

Swiss Steak

I have served this for years to a variety of very picky eaters…they all loved it! Buttery mashed potatoes are delicious alongside.

2 lbs. boneless beef round steak, cut into 6 serving pieces
1.1-oz. pkg. beefy onion soup mix
3 c. onion, sliced
28-oz. can diced tomatoes, undrained
3 T. all-purpose flour
1 c. water
Garnish: fresh parlsey, minced

Arrange steak in a slow cooker. Sprinkle soup mix over steak; arrange onion slices all around. Top with tomatoes. Cover and cook on low setting for 8 hours or on high setting for 4 hours. Remove steak and vegetables to a serving dish; set aside. Mix together flour and water in a small bowl; add to slow cooker and stir until thickened. Spoon gravy over steak to serve. Sprinkle with parsley. Serves 4 to 6.

Jean Carter
Rockledge, FL

make it easy

Add zest to a soup or stew recipe…easy! Just choose a seasoned variety of canned diced tomatoes such as Italian or Mexican.

Pork Chops à la Orange

These pork chops have the taste of a tropical luau, and they're made so easily in the slow cooker!

3 lbs. pork chops
salt and pepper to taste
2 c. orange juice
2 11-oz. cans mandarin
  oranges, drained

8-oz. can pineapple tidbits,
  drained
cooked egg noodles

Sprinkle pork chops with salt and pepper; place in a slow cooker. Pour orange juice over pork. Cover and cook on low setting for 6 to 8 hours or on high setting for 3 to 4 hours. About 30 minutes before serving, add oranges and pineapple; cover and continue cooking just until warm. Serve with cooked noodles. Serves 6 to 8.

Rogene Rogers
Bemidji, MN

Spiced Apple Pork Chops

4 1¼-inch thick pork chops
  (about 3 lbs.)
1 t. salt, divided
½ t. pepper
1¾ c. onion, chopped
2 c. water

2 5-oz. pkgs. dried apples
½ c. raisins
½ c. brown sugar, packed
1 T. cinnamon
½ t. ground cloves
½ t. ground ginger

Sprinkle pork with ½ teaspoon salt and pepper. Heat a large non-stick skillet over medium-high heat. Add pork to skillet; cook 3 minutes on each side, or until browned. Transfer pork to a lightly greased slow cooker, reserving drippings in pan. Sauté onion in drippings 3 minutes, or until tender. Add onion, remaining ½ teaspoon salt, water and remaining ingredients to pork in slow cooker. Cover and cook on low setting for 6 hours. Serves 4.

Cranberry Pork Chops

6 pork chops
½ t. salt
pepper to taste
16-oz. can jellied cranberry
  sauce
½ c. cranberry juice cocktail
  or apple juice

¼ c. sugar
2 T. spicy mustard
¼ c. cold water
2 T. cornstarch

"One of our favorite meals! It is so easy to prepare, but it looks and tastes like you put a lot of time into it."

—Jill

Season pork chops with salt and pepper; place in a slow cooker. Combine cranberry sauce, juice, sugar and mustard in a bowl; pour over pork chops. Cover and cook on high setting for 6 to 8 hours. Shortly before serving time, remove pork chops to a platter; keep warm. Combine cold water and cornstarch in a saucepan. Cook over medium heat, stirring continuously, until mixture becomes thick. Add liquid from slow cooker to saucepan and boil until thickened. Serve pork chops with sauce. Serves 6.

Jill Ball
Highland, UT

Homestyle Pork Chops

Makes lots of delicious gravy to serve over rice or potatoes.

½ c. all-purpose flour
1½ t. dry mustard
½ t. salt
½ t. garlic powder

6 pork chops
2 T. oil
10½-oz. can chicken broth

Combine flour, mustard, salt and garlic powder in a shallow bowl. Coat pork chops in mixture; set aside any remaining mixture. Brown pork chops in oil in a skillet over medium-high heat; drain. Stir together broth and remaining flour mixture in a slow cooker; add pork chops. Cover and cook on high setting for 2½ hours. Serves 6.

Delina Jenkins
Hamilton, GA

slow-cooker secrets

Try using cream of chicken, celery or mushroom soup instead of milk or cream when adapting a recipe to slow cooking. The soup can cook for a long time without curdling.

mess-free coating

An easy way to coat food with a breading is to use a plastic zipping bag. Place the flour mixture in the bag and add the food to be coated, a few pieces at a time. Close the bag and shake well.

Colorado Pork Chops
Linda Wolfe (Westminster, CO)

These tasty little pork chops feature all the flavors of your favorite Mexican restaurant. Shred the meat and serve with soft flour tortillas or crispy corn tortilla chips, if desired.

6 pork chops
15-oz. can chili beans with chili sauce
1½ c. salsa

1 c. corn
Optional: green chiles to taste
3 to 4 c. cooked rice

Layer all ingredients except rice in order given in a slow cooker. Cover and cook on low setting for 5 hours or on high setting for 2½ hours. Serve over cooked rice. Serves 6.

Thai-Style Ribs

3½ lbs. pork baby back ribs, racks cut in half
11.5-oz. can frozen orange-pineapple-apple juice concentrate, thawed
¾ c. soy sauce
¼ c. creamy peanut butter
¼ c. fresh cilantro, minced
2 T. fresh ginger, peeled and minced
1 clove garlic, pressed
2 t. sugar
Garnish: fresh cilantro sprigs

Place ribs in a large shallow dish or plastic zipping bag. Whisk together remaining ingredients except garnish in a small bowl. Reserve ¾ cup mixture in refrigerator for dipping. Pour remaining mixture over ribs; cover or seal and chill 8 hours, turning occasionally. Remove ribs from marinade, discarding marinade. Place one rack of ribs in bottom of a slow cooker; stand remaining rib racks on their sides around edges of slow cooker. Cover and cook on high setting for one hour. Reduce heat to low setting; continue to cook for 5 hours. Place reserved ¾ cup sauce in a one-cup glass measuring cup; microwave, uncovered, on high one to 1½ minutes, until thoroughly heated, stirring once. Serve with ribs. Garnish with cilantro sprigs. Serves 2 to 4.

storing fresh herbs

When storing a bunch of fresh herbs, wrap the stems in a damp paper towel and store them in a plastic zipping bag. Wash the herbs just before using; then pat them dry with a paper towel.

Honey-Mustard Short Ribs

If your grocer or butcher carries boneless short ribs, cooking time can be reduced by about an hour.

3 to 4 lbs. bone-in beef short ribs
salt and pepper to taste
1 c. hickory smoke-flavored barbecue sauce
3 T. honey
1 T. Dijon mustard
3 cloves garlic, minced
2 T. cornstarch
2 T. cold water

Sprinkle ribs with salt and pepper; place in a slow cooker and set aside. Combine barbecue sauce, honey, mustard, garlic and additional salt and pepper, if desired, in a small bowl; pour over ribs. Cover and cook on low setting for 6 to 7 hours. During the last 30 minutes of cooking, whisk cornstarch into water in a small bowl; add to slow cooker, stirring until sauce is thickened. Serves 4.

David Wink
Marion, OH

slow-cooker secrets

Slow cookers are so handy that you may want more than one! A 5½- or 6-quart model is just right for families and potlucks…a smaller 3-quart one will cook for two or can be used for dips and sauces.

Tangy Pork Ribs

¼ c. soy sauce
⅓ c. orange marmalade
3 T. catsup
2 cloves garlic, minced
3 to 4 lbs. country-style pork ribs

Combine soy sauce, marmalade, catsup and garlic in a small bowl. Pour half into a slow cooker; top with ribs and drizzle with remaining sauce. Cover and cook on low setting for 6 hours, or until tender. Serves 6 to 8.

Jo Ann
Gooseberry Patch

"Thick, country-style ribs are always a family favorite…now this is the only way I serve them."

—Jo Ann

Farmhouse Pork & Sauerkraut

This dish really warms you up on those chilly days. The apple and potato disappear into the cheese soup as they cook, making a delicious sauce.

4-lb. pork loin roast
1 T. oil
27-oz. can sauerkraut, drained
  and rinsed
¼ c. water
1 onion, sliced
1 potato, peeled and sliced
10¾-oz. can Cheddar cheese
  soup

1 T. caraway seed
1 Granny Smith apple, peeled,
  cored and sliced
salt and pepper to taste
Garnish: fresh parsley,
  chopped

Brown pork on all sides in oil in a skillet over medium heat; place in a slow cooker. Combine remaining ingredients except salt, pepper and garnish in a large bowl. Pour over roast; cover and cook on low setting for 10 hours. Season pork with salt and pepper and garnish with chopped parsley before serving. Serves 6.

Diane Cohen
Kennesaw, GA

Pork Tenderloins

This couldn't be easier to fix!

2 1-lb. pork tenderloins
10¾-oz. can cream of
  mushroom soup
10¾-oz. can golden mushroom
  soup

10¾-oz. can French onion
  soup

Arrange pork in a slow cooker. Whisk soups together in a bowl; pour over pork. Cover and cook on low setting for 4 to 5 hours, until pork is tender. Serves 4 to 6.

Connie Spangler
Palm Bay, FL

Pork Marengo

Pork Marengo

In a hurry? Don't brown the pork and onion…this dish will still be tasty!

2 lbs. boneless pork shoulder, cubed
1 yellow onion, chopped
2 T. oil
14½-oz. can diced tomatoes, undrained
1 c. sliced mushrooms
1 t. chicken bouillon granules
1 t. dried marjoram
½ t. dried thyme
⅛ t. pepper
⅓ c. cold water
3 T. all-purpose flour
salt and pepper to taste
cooked rice or pasta
Garnish: fresh oregano

Cook pork cubes and onion in oil in a skillet over medium heat until browned. Drain and place in a slow cooker; set aside. Combine tomatoes, mushrooms, bouillon and seasonings in skillet. Pour over pork. Cover and cook on low setting for 8 hours. Blend water into flour in a small bowl; stir into pork. Add salt and pepper. Increase heat to high setting and cook, uncovered, for 15 to 20 minutes, until thickened, stirring occasionally. Serve over cooked rice or pasta. Garnish with oregano. Serves 4 to 6.

Penny Sherman
Cumming, GA

slow-cooker secrets

Adapt a favorite family recipe to slow cooking…simple! Cut liquid in half and convert simmering or baking time as follows:

35 to 45 minutes =
6 to 8 hours on low or
3 to 4 hours on high

one to 3 hours =
8 to 10 hours on low or
4 to 6 hours on high

Saucy Potatoes + Ham

A satisfying main dish or a tasty side…perfect either way for a carry-in dinner.

4 c. potatoes, peeled and thinly sliced
1 c. onion, sliced
10¾-oz. can cream of celery soup
12-oz. can evaporated milk
2 T. butter
½ t. salt
¼ t. pepper
1½ c. cooked ham, cubed

Combine all ingredients except ham in a slow cooker. Cover and cook on high setting for one hour. Stir in ham. Reduce heat to low setting; cover and cook for 6 to 8 hours, until potatoes are tender. Serves 4 to 6.

Janine Edwards-Klinker
Gordonville, TX

Cheesy Ham + Noodles

This family-friendly pasta dish is adaptable...use your favorite type of frozen vegetable and substitute whipping cream and Gruyère cheese for the half-and-half and Swiss cheese.

12-oz. pkg. linguine pasta, uncooked
3 c. half-and-half
2 c. shredded Swiss cheese, divided
1 c. frozen peas
1 T. Dijon mustard
12-oz. lean ham steak, chopped
10-oz. container refrigerated Alfredo sauce

Cook linguine in boiling water in a 4-quart saucepan for 5 minutes; drain. Transfer linguine to a lightly greased slow cooker. Add half-and-half, one cup cheese and remaining ingredients, stirring gently to blend. Sprinkle with remaining one cup cheese. Cover and cook on low setting for 3 hours, or until linguine is tender. Serves 6.

Country-Style Ham au Gratin

Ham and cheese just seem to go together...and never better than in this creamy dish.

2 c. cooked ham, diced
2 c. milk
1 c. boiling water
10¾-oz. can Cheddar cheese
 soup
7.8-oz. pkg. cheesy scalloped
 potato mix
2 11-oz. cans sweet corn &
 diced peppers, drained

Combine all ingredients in a slow cooker; mix well. Cover and cook on low setting for 8 to 9 hours. Serves 4 to 6.

Joshua Logan
Corpus Christi, TX

Sausage, Red Beans + Rice

16-oz. pkg. dried red beans
1 lb. smoked sausage, sliced
1 c. onion, chopped
5 c. water
¾ c. fresh parsley, chopped
1 t. salt
½ t. dried oregano
½ t. dried thyme
⅛ t. cayenne pepper
3 cloves garlic, minced
hot cooked rice
hot pepper sauce
Garnish: green onions,
 chopped

Rinse and sort beans according to package directions. Cover with water 2 inches above beans; let soak 8 hours. Drain and place in a slow cooker. Sauté sausage and onion in a large skillet over medium-high heat 5 minutes, or until sausage is browned and onion is tender. Stir sausage mixture, water, parsley, salt, oregano, thyme, cayenne pepper and garlic into beans. Cover and cook on low setting for 8 hours. Mash beans with a potato masher or the back of a spoon to desired consistency. Serve with rice and hot pepper sauce; sprinkle with green onions. Serves 8.

Crock o' Brats

Serve with hearty rye bread and homestyle applesauce sprinkled with cinnamon.

slow-cooker secrets

There's usually no need for stirring! A slow cooker surrounds food with even heat...it won't scorch on the bottom. If you do stir, be sure to put the lid back on as quickly as possible.

20-oz. pkg. bratwurst
5 potatoes, peeled and cubed
1 tart apple, peeled, cored and cubed
1 onion, chopped
¼ c. brown sugar, packed
½ t. salt
27-oz. can sauerkraut, drained

Brown bratwurst in a large skillet over medium heat; reserve drippings. Slice bratwurst into one-inch pieces; set aside. Combine remaining ingredients in a slow cooker. Stir in bratwurst slices with pan drippings. Cover and cook on high setting for 4 to 6 hours, until potatoes are tender. Serves 6.

Naomi Cooper
Delaware, OH

Chicken + Dumplings

With a slow cooker, you can serve your family a homestyle dinner even after a busy day away from home.

1½ lbs. boneless, skinless chicken breasts, cubed
2 potatoes, cubed
2 c. baby carrots
2 stalks celery, sliced
2 10¾-oz. cans cream of chicken soup
1 c. water
1 t. dried thyme
¼ t. pepper
2 c. biscuit baking mix
⅔ c. milk

Place chicken, potatoes, carrots and celery in a slow cooker. Combine soup, water, thyme and pepper in a medium bowl; pour over chicken mixture. Cover and cook on low setting 7 to 8 hours, until juices run clear when chicken is pierced. Mix together baking mix and milk in a bowl; drop into slow cooker by large spoonfuls. Tilt lid to vent and cook on high setting 30 minutes, or until dumplings are cooked in center. Serves 8.

Rhonda Reeder
Ellicott City, MD

Chicken-Netti

The kids will love this...so will the grown-ups!

16-oz. pkg. spaghetti, cooked
2 c. chicken broth
10¾-oz. can cream of mushroom soup
10¾-oz. can cream of chicken soup
4 to 6 green onions, chopped
16-oz. pkg. pasteurized process cheese spread, cubed
4 boneless, skinless chicken breasts, cooked and cubed
⅛ t. celery salt
⅛ t. pepper

Combine all ingredients in a slow cooker. Cover and cook on low setting for 2 to 3 hours, stirring frequently, until warmed through. Serves 8 to 10.

Lynn Knepp
Montgomery, IN

Chicken Cacciatore

When making a garden-fresh recipe like this one, use a mixture of veggies from the garden...just as tasty with any favorite combinations!

"I'm not an accomplished cook, but every time I make this, my family just swoons! It is tasty any time of the year and is so easy."

—Mary

1 lb. boneless, skinless chicken breasts
26-oz. jar chunky garden vegetable spaghetti sauce
1 zucchini, chopped
1 green pepper, chopped
1 sweet onion, chopped
cooked wide egg noodles or spaghetti
Garnish: sliced black olives, shredded Parmesan cheese

Place chicken in a slow cooker; pour sauce over top. Add vegetables. Cover and cook on low setting for 6 to 8 hours. Spoon over egg noodles or spaghetti. Garnish with black olives and Parmesan cheese. Serves 4.

Mary Whitacre
Mount Vernon, OH

Chicken Cacciatore

Autumn Nutmeg Chicken

This is so creamy and yummy! The nutmeg lends a sweetness that is complemented by the rosemary, sage and thyme.

slow-cooker secrets

Slow cookers work best when filled half to two-thirds full with ingredients.

6 boneless, skinless chicken breasts
1 to 2 T. oil
1 onion, chopped
¼ c. fresh parsley, minced
2 10¾-oz. cans cream of mushroom soup
½ c. sour cream
½ c. milk
1 T. nutmeg
¼ t. dried rosemary
¼ t. dried sage
¼ t. dried thyme
cooked rice

Brown chicken in oil in a skillet over medium heat; reserve drippings. Arrange chicken in a slow cooker; set aside. Sauté onion and parsley in reserved drippings until onion is tender. Add remaining ingredients except rice; mix well and pour over chicken. Cover and cook on low setting for 5 hours, or until juices run clear when chicken is pierced. Serve over cooked rice. Serves 6.

Marilyn Morel
Keene, NH

Garlicky Bacon Chicken

Easy and elegant…makes a divine creamy sauce to serve on top of wild rice.

8 slices bacon
8 boneless, skinless chicken breasts
2 10¾-oz. cans cream of mushroom with roasted garlic soup
1 c. sour cream
½ c. all-purpose flour

Wrap one slice of bacon around each chicken breast and place in a slow cooker. Whisk together soup, sour cream and flour in a medium bowl. Pour over chicken. Cover and cook on low setting for 6 to 8 hours. Transfer to a broiler pan and broil 5 minutes to crisp bacon, if desired. Serves 8.

Lisa Robason
Corpus Christi, TX

slow-cooker secrets

Baked potatoes are yummy with any dish and, with a slow cooker, so easy to prepare! Simply use a fork to pierce 10 to 12 baking potatoes and wrap each in aluminum foil. Arrange them in a slow cooker, cover and cook on high setting for 2½ to 4 hours, until tender.

Aloha Chicken

Aloha Chicken

4 lbs. boneless, skinless chicken breasts
20-oz. can pineapple chunks, undrained
11-oz. can mandarin oranges, drained
1 green or red pepper, chopped
¼ c. onion, chopped
1 clove garlic, minced
1 T. soy sauce
1 t. fresh ginger, peeled and grated
Garnish: chopped green onions

Arrange chicken in a slow cooker; set aside. Combine remaining ingredients except garnish in a bowl; pour over chicken. Cover and cook on low setting for 8 to 10 hours. Cut chicken into strips. Garnish with green onions. Serves 8 to 10.

Yvonne Van Brimmer
Apple Valley, CA

"I like to serve this over steamed rice, sprinkled with fresh coconut flakes for an extra taste of the tropics."

—Yvonne

Tammy's Italian Chicken

Everyone loves this quick & easy dish! My son scored a thumbs-up from the other firefighters on his crew when it was his turn to cook, and my sister-in-law got rave reviews when she served it to her son's high school football team.

2½ lbs. chicken breasts
1½-oz. pkg. spaghetti sauce mix
14½-oz. can diced tomatoes, undrained
8-oz. can tomato sauce
cooked penne pasta
Garnish: grated Parmesan cheese

Arrange chicken in a slow cooker. Sprinkle with sauce mix; add tomatoes and tomato sauce. Cover and cook on low setting for 4 to 5 hours. Serve over penne pasta; sprinkle with Parmesan cheese. Serves 4 to 6.

Julie Klum
Lake Oswego, OR

slow-cooker secrets

Spray the inside of your slow cooker with non-stick vegetable spray before adding ingredients…clean-up will be a snap!

Mozzarella Chicken + Orzo

Dress this up with anything you like…mushrooms, black olives and garlic all add terrific flavor.

8 boneless, skinless chicken
   breasts
¼ t. salt
⅛ t. pepper
1 onion, chopped
2 green peppers, coarsely
   chopped

2 c. pasta sauce
1 c. shredded mozzarella
   cheese
cooked orzo pasta or rice

Place chicken in a slow cooker; sprinkle with salt and pepper. Top with onion and green peppers; pour pasta sauce over top. Cover and cook on low setting for 4 to 5 hours. Stir well and sprinkle with cheese. Let stand for 5 minutes, or until cheese is melted. Serve over cooked pasta or rice. Serves 8.

Jennifer Martineau
Delaware, OH

Poppy Seed Chicken

Don't be tempted to sprinkle on the cracker-crumb mixture while the chicken is in the slow cooker…condensation will make the topping soggy.

6 boneless, skinless chicken breasts
2 10¾-oz. cans cream of chicken soup
1 c. milk
1 T. poppy seed
36 round buttery crackers, crushed
¼ c. butter, melted

Place chicken in a lightly greased slow cooker. Whisk together soup, milk and poppy seed in a medium bowl; pour over chicken. Cover and cook on high setting for one hour. Reduce heat to low setting and cook, covered, 3 hours. Combine cracker crumbs and butter in a bowl, stirring until crumbs are moistened. Sprinkle over chicken just before serving. Serves 6.

Maple Praline Chicken

Jill Valentine (Jackson, Tennessee)

6 boneless, skinless chicken
  breasts
2 T. Cajun seasoning
¼ c. butter
½ c. maple syrup

2 T. brown sugar, packed
1 c. chopped pecans
6-oz. pkg. long-grain and wild rice,
  cooked

Sprinkle chicken with Cajun seasoning. Melt butter in a skillet over medium-high heat; cook chicken in butter until golden. Arrange chicken in a slow cooker. Mix together syrup, brown sugar and pecans in a small bowl; pour over chicken. Cover and cook on low setting for 6 to 8 hours. Serve with cooked rice. Serves 6.

Company Chicken Dijon

Just toss the ingredients in the slow cooker in the morning and then arrive home to a delicious dinner. Serve with cooked rice and steamed, buttered broccoli spears...mmm!

4 to 6 boneless, skinless
  chicken breasts
10¾-oz. can cream of
  mushroom soup

2 T. Dijon mustard
2 T. water
2 t. cornstarch
⅛ t. pepper

Place chicken breasts in a slow cooker. Combine remaining ingredients in a bowl and spoon over chicken. Cover and cook on low setting for 6 to 8 hours. Serves 4 to 6.

Kay Marone
Des Moines, IA

refreshing lemonade

Serve up icy lemonade in sugar-rimmed frosty glasses! Chill tall tumblers in the fridge. At serving time, moisten rims with lemon juice or water and dip into a dish of sparkling sugar. Carefully pour in chilled lemonade. It's perfect for guests.

Sesame Chicken

1¼ c. chicken broth
½ c. brown sugar, packed
¼ c. cornstarch
2 T. rice vinegar
2 T. soy sauce
2 T. sweet chili sauce
2 T. honey
2 t. dark sesame oil
1½ lbs. boneless, skinless
   chicken breasts, cut into
   1-inch pieces
2 c. sugar snap peas
2 c. crinkle-cut carrots
1½ T. sesame seed, toasted
hot cooked rice
Garnish: chopped green onions

Whisk together broth, brown sugar, cornstarch, vinegar, soy sauce, chili sauce, honey and oil in a slow cooker. Stir in chicken. Cover and cook on high setting for 2½ hours, or until juices run clear when chicken is pierced, stirring after 1½ hours. Steam sugar snap peas and carrots over boiling water until tender. Stir vegetable mixture and sesame seed into slow cooker. Serve over hot cooked rice. Garnish with green onions. Serves 4 to 6.

Mom's Company Chicken

"The flavors come together to make this chicken dish one I serve again and again...to rave reviews!"

—Amanda

2 lbs. boneless, skinless
   chicken thighs
3 cloves garlic, minced
1 onion, chopped
½ c. sweet-and-sour sauce
½ c. barbecue sauce
cooked rice or couscous

Combine all ingredients except rice or couscous in a slow cooker. Cover and cook on low setting for 8 to 9 hours, until juices run clear when chicken is pierced. Serve over cooked rice or couscous. Serves 6.

Amanda Lusignolo
Columbus, OH

Sesame Chicken

Chicken Chow Mein

1 red pepper, cut into strips
2 lbs. chicken breast tenders
   or 2 lbs. boneless, skinless
   chicken breasts, cut into strips
½ t. pepper
1 T. oil
½ c. lite soy sauce
¼ c. oyster sauce
1 T. dark sesame oil
2 t. fresh ginger, peeled and
   grated
1 T. cornstarch

2 T. water
2 c. frozen broccoli cuts
1 c. frozen fully cooked
   shelled edamame (green
   soybeans)
2 8-oz. cans sliced water
   chestnuts, drained
hot cooked rice
3 green onions, diagonally
   sliced
Optional: 3-oz. can chow mein
   noodles

Place pepper strips in a lightly greased slow cooker. Sprinkle chicken with pepper. Heat vegetable oil in a large non-stick skillet over medium-high heat. Cook chicken in oil 2 minutes on each side; transfer to slow cooker. Combine soy sauce, oyster sauce, sesame oil and ginger in a small bowl; pour over chicken in slow cooker. Cover and cook on low setting for 2 hours. Combine cornstarch and water in a small bowl, stirring until smooth. Stir into mixture in slow cooker. Stir in frozen broccoli, frozen edamame and water chestnuts. Cover and cook on low setting for one hour. Serve over cooked rice. Sprinkle with green onions. Top with chow mein noodles, if desired. Serves 6 to 8.

sharing the news

Prop a mini chalkboard next to the slow cooker…it's just right for announcing what's for dinner and what time it will be ready.

Oriental Chicken

A garnish of minced fresh chives is tasty on servings of this sweet-and-sour chicken dish.

2 lbs. boneless, skinless
chicken thighs, cut into
bite-size pieces
2 12-oz. jars sweet-and-sour
sauce

16-oz. pkg. frozen broccoli,
carrots and peppers blend,
thawed and drained

Combine chicken and sauce in a slow cooker. Cover and cook on low setting for 7 to 8 hours. Stir in vegetables. Increase heat to high setting; cover and cook for 10 to 15 minutes, until vegetables are crisp-tender. Serves 6 to 8.

Sherry Gordon
Arlington Heights, IL

slow-cooker secrets

For easy, no-fuss cleaning, transfer your dinner to a serving plate. Fill the empty slow cooker with warm, soapy water and let it soak.

Sweet + Spicy Chicken

The sweetness of the marmalade blends with the curry and cayenne to make this amazing slow-cooker chicken!

4 to 6 boneless, skinless
chicken breasts
salt and pepper to taste
12-oz. jar orange marmalade

½ c. chicken broth
1½ t. curry powder
½ t. cayenne pepper
Optional: ⅛ t. ground ginger

Sprinkle chicken with salt and pepper; place in a slow cooker. Whisk together marmalade, broth and spices in a bowl. Pour over chicken. Cover and cook on low setting for 5 to 7 hours or on high setting for 3 to 4 hours, turning chicken halfway through cooking. Serves 4 to 6.

Annette Ingram
Grand Rapids, MI

Chicken Cordon Bleu

"I always used to fix this dish in the oven when we lived up north. When we moved to Florida, I was really glad to find a slow-cooker version so I didn't have to heat up the kitchen."

—Beth

4 to 6 boneless, skinless chicken breasts
4 to 6 slices deli ham
4 to 6 slices Swiss cheese
10¾-oz. can cream of mushroom soup
¼ c. milk
cooked egg noodles
Garnish: paprika

Place each chicken breast between 2 pieces of wax paper; flatten with a meat mallet. Remove wax paper. Top with a slice of ham and a slice of cheese. Roll up and secure with wooden toothpicks. Arrange chicken rolls in a slow cooker, making 2 layers if necessary. Blend soup and milk in a bowl; pour over chicken. Cover and cook on low setting for 4 hours, or until juices run clear when chicken is pierced. Serve chicken rolls over cooked noodles. Top with sauce from slow cooker; sprinkle with paprika. Serves 4 to 6.

Beth Kramer
Port Saint Lucie, FL

Anne's Chicken Burritos

6 boneless, skinless chicken
  breasts
15¼-oz. can corn, drained
16-oz. can black beans, drained
  and rinsed

16-oz. jar salsa
6 to 8 10-inch flour tortillas
Garnish: shredded Cheddar
  cheese, salsa, chopped fresh
  cilantro

Combine chicken, corn, beans and salsa in a slow cooker. Cover and
cook on low setting for 8 to 10 hours or on high setting for 4 to 6 hours.
Shred chicken; stir back into slow cooker. Roll up in tortillas; garnish as
desired. Serves 6 to 8.

*"Anne is a friend of
mine who gave me
this easy slow-cooker
recipe...we love it
more and more each
time we make it!"*

—Jennifer

Jennifer Sievers
Roselle, IL

Lemon-Rosemary Chicken

Rather than removing the slow-cooker lid to check on the chicken, it's best to gently tap the lid to release the condensation so you can see inside.

4-lb. chicken
1 lemon, halved
3 sprigs fresh rosemary
2 cloves garlic, peeled
3 T. butter, divided
salt and pepper to taste
Garnish: lemon wedges, fresh rosemary sprigs

Rinse chicken and pat dry. Place lemon halves, 3 rosemary sprigs, garlic and 2 tablespoons butter inside cavity of chicken. Fold wing tips under chicken; tie legs together with kitchen string. Sprinkle chicken with salt and pepper. Place chicken, breast-side up, on a small rack inside an oval slow cooker. Cover and cook on high setting for 4 to 4½ hours, until an instant-read meat thermometer inserted into thigh registers 165 degrees. Melt remaining one tablespoon butter in a small bowl. Transfer chicken, breast-side up, to an aluminum foil-lined baking sheet. Brush chicken with melted butter; broil for 2 to 3 minutes to brown skin. Let stand 10 minutes on a cutting board before carving and serving. Garnish with lemon wedges and rosemary sprigs. Serves 4.

Peach-Ginger Wings

4 lbs. halved chicken wings (about 32 wing pieces)
1 c. peach preserves
½ c. soy sauce
2 T. fresh ginger, peeled and grated
1 T. frozen limeade concentrate, thawed
1 T. garlic, minced
¼ t. hot pepper sauce

Place wings on a lightly greased rack in a lightly greased broiler pan. Broil 3 inches from heat for 14 minutes, or until browned. Transfer wings to a lightly greased slow cooker. Stir together preserves and remaining ingredients in a small bowl. Pour peach mixture over wings. Cover and cook on low setting for 4 hours. Serve with sauce. Serves 4 to 6.

make it easy

Use a vegetable peeler to remove skin and reveal the yellow flesh of fresh ginger. For grated ginger, rub a peeled piece of ginger across a fine grater.

Peach-Ginger
Wings

Honey-BBQ
Chicken Wings

Honey-BBQ Chicken Wings

Add a side of steamed rice and veggies for a tasty no-fuss meal.

3 lbs. chicken wings
salt and pepper to taste
1 c. honey
¼ c. barbecue sauce
¼ c. teriyaki sauce
¼ c. soy sauce
2 T. oil
1 clove garlic, minced
Garnish: green onions,
   chopped

Arrange chicken wings on a lightly greased broiler pan; sprinkle with salt and pepper. Broil for 12 to 15 minutes on each side, until golden. Transfer wings to a slow cooker. Combine remaining ingredients except garnish in a bowl and pour over wings. Cover and cook on low setting for 4 hours or on high setting for 2 hours. Garnish with green onions. Serve with sauce. Serves 4 to 6.

Kendall Hale
Lynn, MA

Easiest-Ever Turkey Dinner

What a wonderful dinner for a small gathering…it can even cook while you're catching up and sharing laughs with your holiday company.

3 potatoes, peeled and cubed
3 skinless turkey thighs
12-oz. jar homestyle turkey
   gravy
1 t. dried parsley
½ t. dried thyme
⅛ t. pepper

Arrange potatoes in a slow cooker; place turkey on top. Stir together gravy and seasonings in a bowl; pour over turkey. Cover and cook on low setting for 8 to 10 hours, until juices run clear when turkey is pierced. Remove turkey and potatoes from slow cooker using a slotted spoon. Stir gravy and serve with turkey. Serves 6.

Claire Bertram
Lexington, KY

Maple-Glazed Turkey Breast

Sprinkle in sweetened dried cranberries for an extra burst of color and flavor.

6-oz. pkg. long-grain and wild
  rice, uncooked
1¼ c. water
1-lb. turkey breast

¼ c. maple syrup
½ c. chopped walnuts
½ t. cinnamon

Mix together uncooked rice, seasoning packet from rice and water in a 4-quart slow cooker. Place turkey breast, skin-side up, on rice mixture. Drizzle with syrup; sprinkle with walnuts and cinnamon. Cover and cook on low setting for 4 to 5 hours, until a meat thermometer inserted into breast registers 165 degrees. Let stand 10 minutes before slicing. Serves 4.

Eleanor Paternoster
Bridgeport, CT

Turkey + Dressing

"I like to start this before I leave for work...all I have to do when I get home is slice and serve!"

—Geneva

8-oz. pkg. stuffing mix
½ c. hot water
2 T. butter, softened
1 onion, chopped
½ c. celery, chopped
¼ c. sweetened dried
  cranberries

3-lb. boneless turkey breast
¼ t. dried basil
½ t. salt
½ t. pepper

Coat the inside of a 4-quart slow cooker with non-stick vegetable spray; spoon in dry stuffing mix. Add water, butter, onion, celery and cranberries; mix well. Sprinkle turkey breast with basil, salt and pepper and place over stuffing mixture. Cover and cook on low setting for 6 to 7 hours. Remove turkey from slow cooker, slice and set aside. Gently stir the stuffing and let stand for 5 minutes. Transfer stuffing to a platter and top with sliced turkey. Serves 6 to 8.

Geneva Rogers
Gillette, WY

Maple-Glazed
Turkey Breast

Pot Roast & Sweet
Potatoes, page 60

mouthwatering roasts

Enjoy these comfort foods at their finest! Mom's Fall-Apart Sunday Roast lives up to its name. Pot Roast & Sweet Potatoes has a hint of cinnamon. Apple-Glazed Pork Roast offers autumn flavors year 'round. And there's no need to heat up the oven when easy Sweet & Spicy Country Ham can bake in the slow cooker.

Mom's Fall-Apart Sunday Roast

"My mom would always put this roast into the slow cooker early on Sunday mornings, before getting ready for church. When we came home around noon, the whole house smelled wonderful!"

—Karla

3-lb. boneless beef chuck roast
salt, pepper and garlic powder
  to taste
1 to 2 T. oil
4 to 6 potatoes, peeled and
  quartered

1 to 2 onions, quartered
3 to 4 carrots, peeled and cut
  into chunks
3 14½-oz. cans green beans,
  drained and liquid reserved

Sprinkle roast generously with salt, pepper and garlic powder. Heat oil in a skillet over medium-high heat; brown roast on all sides. Place potatoes in a slow cooker; place roast on top of potatoes. Add onions, carrots and green beans, sprinkling to taste with additional salt, pepper and garlic powder. Add enough of reserved liquid from beans to cover ingredients about halfway. Cover and cook on low setting for 6 to 8 hours. Serves 6.

Karla Neese
Edmond, OK

homestyle gravy

Make gravy after a slow-cooked roast is done…it's easy. Set aside roast, leaving juices in the slow cooker. Stir up a smooth paste of ¼ cup cold water and ¼ cup cornstarch or all-purpose flour. Pour it into the slow cooker, stir well and set on high. In about 15 minutes, the gravy will come to a boil…it's ready to serve!

Italian-Style Pot Roast

Rosemary Kerns (Saint Joseph, MO)

1 onion, sliced
3 cloves garlic, minced
28-oz. can crushed tomatoes
2 T. balsamic vinegar
1 T. Worcestershire sauce

1 T. Italian seasoning
2 t. brown sugar, packed
salt and pepper to taste
2 to 3-lb. beef chuck roast

Blend together all ingredients except roast in a bowl. Pour half the mixture into a slow cooker and add roast; pour remaining mixture over top. Cover and cook on low setting for 6 to 8 hours. Serves 6.

Pot Roast + Sweet Potatoes

1½ to 2-lb. boneless beef chuck roast
2 T. oil
1 onion, thinly sliced
3 sweet potatoes, peeled and quartered
⅔ c. beef broth
¾ t. celery salt
¼ t. salt
¼ t. pepper
¼ t. cinnamon
1 T. cornstarch
2 T. cold water

Brown roast in hot oil in a skillet over medium-high heat; drain. Place onion and potatoes in slow cooker; top with roast. Combine broth and seasonings in a small bowl; pour over roast. Cover and cook on low setting for 7 to 8 hours. Place roast and vegetables on a serving platter; keep warm. Combine cornstarch and water in a small saucepan; add one cup of juices from slow cooker. Cook and stir over medium heat until thickened and bubbly; continue cooking and stirring 2 more minutes. Serve gravy with roast. Serves 4.

Barbara Schmeckpeper
Minooka, IL

Savory Merlot Pot Roast

For a thicker gravy, combine one tablespoon cornstarch and 2 tablespoons water. Add to gravy in slow cooker once roast is removed. Cook, uncovered, for 15 minutes, or until desired thickness.

3 to 4-lb. beef chuck roast
½ t. meat tenderizer
pepper to taste
1 t. olive oil
10¾-oz. can cream of mushroom soup
1½-oz. pkg. onion soup mix
½ c. merlot wine or beef broth

Sprinkle roast on all sides with tenderizer and pepper. Brown roast in hot oil in a large skillet over medium heat. Transfer to a slow cooker. Combine soup, soup mix and wine; pour over roast. Cover and cook on low setting for 6 to 8 hours. Remove roast to a serving platter; keep warm. Serves 6 to 8.

Heather McClintock
Columbus, OH

Farmhouse Pot Roast
Cherylann Smith (Efland, NC)

3-lb. beef chuck roast
salt and pepper to taste
8-oz. pkg. whole mushrooms
16 new redskin potatoes
½ lb. carrots, peeled and sliced
3 stalks celery, chopped

14-oz. can beef broth
2 c. water
26-oz. can cream of mushroom
  soup

Optional: fresh parsley, chopped

Season roast with salt and pepper and brown on all sides in a skillet over high heat. Place roast in an ungreased slow cooker; top with vegetables. Blend together broth, water and soup in a medium bowl; pour over roast. Cover and cook on low setting for 6 to 8 hours, until roast is very tender. Garnish with parsley, if desired. Serves 6.

Spicy Marinated Eye of Round

3 to 5-lb. beef eye-of-round
  roast
½ t. salt

¼ t. pepper
3 sweet onions, sliced

Sprinkle roast with salt and pepper. Place roast and onions in a slow cooker. Pour Spicy Sauce over roast. Cover and cook on low heat setting for 8 hours. Remove roast; cool slightly and cut into thin slices. Return slices to sauce in slow cooker. Discard bay leaf before serving. Serves 8 to 10.

Spicy Sauce:

2 c. catsup
2 c. water
2 sweet onions, sliced
⅓ c. red wine vinegar
¼ c. brown sugar, packed
2 T. Worcestershire sauce
1 t. dry mustard
1 t. dried oregano

1 t. pepper
½ t. garlic powder
½ t. chili powder
½ t. ground cloves
¼ t. nutmeg
¼ t. hot pepper sauce
1 bay leaf

Combine all ingredients in a bowl. Makes 7 cups.

slow-cooker secrets

All-day slow cooking works wonders on less-tender, inexpensive cuts of beef… arm and chuck roast, rump roast, short ribs, round steak and stew beef cook up juicy and delicious.

decorate from your garden

Tie rolled cloth napkins with ribbon and slip a fresh sprig of sweet-scented thyme under the ribbon…charming!

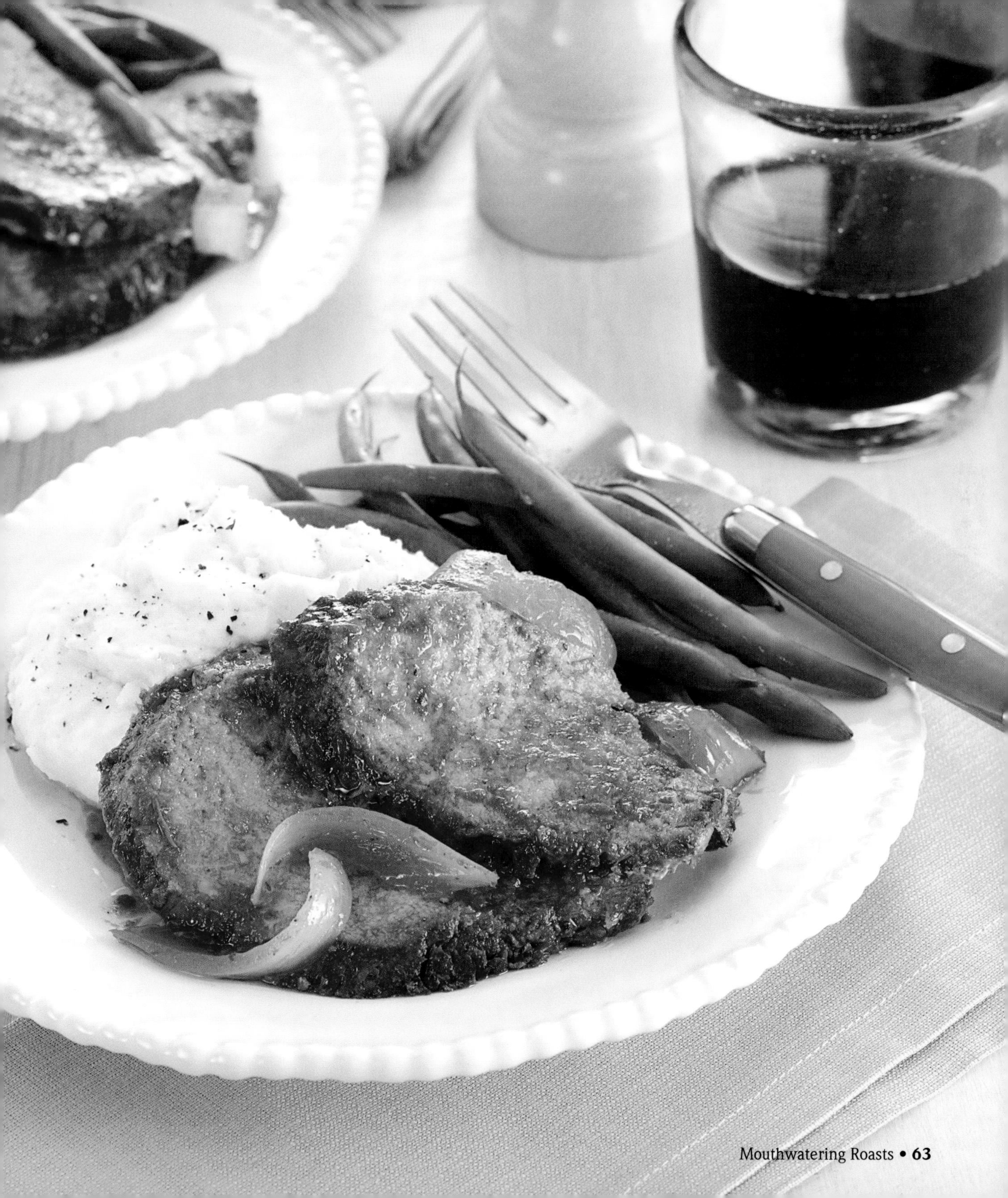

"Smoked" Beef Brisket

So you've planned a cookout for tomorrow, but the weather forecast says rain? No problem…make this delicious smoky-tasting brisket in the slow cooker and have a picnic indoors!

slow-cooker secrets

Set on low, a slow cooker uses about as much energy as a 75-watt lightbulb…less than an electric range uses!

2 to 4-lb. beef brisket or chuck roast
2 T. kosher salt
2 T. pepper, coarsely ground
2 cloves garlic, minced

2 T. smoke-flavored cooking sauce
Optional: barbecue sauce, sandwich buns

Place meat in the center of a length of aluminum foil; rub all over with salt, pepper and garlic. Sprinkle cooking sauce over meat. Wrap aluminum foil around meat to cover completely; seal tightly. Place in a slow cooker; cover and cook on low setting for 8 to 10 hours. Unwrap meat; serve with juices from slow cooker or with barbecue sauce, if desired. Serves 4 to 6.

Joshua Logan
Corpus Christi, TX

Roast for Tacos
Dana Thompson (Gooseberry Patch)

Don't forget to offer all the tasty taco toppers…shredded cheese, sour cream, lettuce, tomatoes, onions and salsa. Olé!

4 to 5-lb. beef chuck roast
1 T. chili powder
1 t. ground cumin
1 t. onion powder
1 t. garlic powder

2 14½-oz. cans Mexican-style stewed tomatoes, undrained
taco shells
Optional: chopped lettuce, tomato and red onion

Place roast in a large slow cooker; sprinkle with seasonings. Pour tomatoes around the roast. Cover and cook on low setting for 8 to 10 hours. Using 2 forks, shred roast and return to slow cooker. Spoon into taco shells. Makes 10 cups.

Cranberry Corned Beef

Cranberry Corned Beef

4-lb. cured corned beef brisket with spice packet
5 large carrots, peeled and cut into 3-inch pieces
1 onion, cut into 6 wedges
14-oz. can whole-berry cranberry sauce
14-oz. can jellied cranberry sauce
2 1-oz. pkgs. onion soup mix
½ c. sour cream
4 t. prepared horseradish
¼ t. pepper
Garnish: fresh parsley, chopped

Trim fat from brisket. Place carrots and onion in a slow cooker; place brisket on top of vegetables. Sprinkle spice packet over brisket. Combine cranberry sauces and soup mix in a bowl. Spoon over brisket. Cover and cook on high setting for one hour. Reduce heat to low setting and cook for 8 hours. Meanwhile, combine sour cream and horseradish in a small bowl. Cover and chill until ready to serve. Transfer brisket to a serving platter. Spoon carrots, onion and, if desired, a little cooking liquid around brisket on platter. Serve with sauce. Sprinkle with pepper. Garnish with parsley. Serves 6 to 8.

slow-cooker secrets

The long, slow-cooking process makes corned beef an ideal meat for the slow cooker. The meat does tend to shrink in the slow cooker, so cooking a large portion such as this works well.

Sally's Supreme Corned Beef

Use a little cornstarch to thicken the broth after removing the brisket from the slow cooker…it makes really good gravy for the noodles.

2 to 3-lb. corned beef brisket
12-oz. bottle chili sauce
1.35-oz. pkg. onion soup mix
12-oz. can cola
cooked egg noodles

Place brisket in a slow cooker. Mix remaining ingredients except noodles in a bowl; pour over brisket. Cover and cook on low setting for 6 to 8 hours. Slice beef and serve over noodles. Serves 4 to 6.

Sally Kohler
Webster, NY

Apple-Glazed Pork Roast

"This roast cooks up so moist! I serve it alongside mashed potatoes and green beans."

—Jen

3 to 4-lb. pork loin roast
salt and pepper to taste
4 to 6 apples, cored and
　quartered

¼ c. apple juice
3 T. brown sugar, packed
1 t. ground ginger

Rub roast with salt and pepper. Brown briefly under broiler to remove excess fat; drain well. Arrange apples in bottom of a slow cooker; place roast on top. Combine remaining ingredients in a small bowl and spoon over roast. Cover and cook on low setting for 10 to 12 hours. Serves 6.

Jen Eveland-Kupp
Temple, PA

Molly's Pork Roast

slow-cooker secrets

Besides the ease of letting a slow cooker do all the work, another advantage is that it uses very little electricity. On average it costs just 21 cents to operate a slow cooker for a total of ten hours!

3-lb. boneless pork roast,
　halved
8-oz. can tomato sauce

¾ c. soy sauce
½ c. sugar
2 t. dry mustard

Place roast in a slow cooker. Combine remaining ingredients in a bowl; pour over roast. Cover and cook on low setting for 8 to 9 hours. Remove roast; slice to serve. Serves 8.

Anna McMaster
Portland, OR

Teriyaki Pork Roast

¾ c. apple juice
2 T. sugar
2 T. soy sauce
1 T. vinegar
1 t. ground ginger

1 t. garlic powder
¼ t. pepper
2 to 3-lb. rolled pork loin roast
3 T. cold water
1½ T. cornstarch

Combine apple juice, sugar, soy sauce, vinegar and seasonings in a slow cooker; mix well. Add roast and turn to coat; place fat-side up. Cover and cook on low setting for 7 to 8 hours or on high setting for 3½ to 4 hours. Shortly before serving, make gravy. Remove roast from slow cooker; place on a platter and keep warm. Strain cooking liquids from slow cooker into a small saucepan; skim fat if necessary. Bring to a boil. Combine water and cornstarch in a small bowl to make a paste; stir into boiling liquid. Cook and stir until thickened. Serve gravy with sliced roast. Serves 4 to 6.

Jane Gates
Saginaw, MI

Sweet & Spicy Country Ham

"This ham brings back memories of Christmas at Grandma's house."

—Claire

6-lb. bone-in country ham
30 whole cloves
3 c. apple cider, divided
1 c. brown sugar, packed
1 c. maple syrup
2 T. cinnamon
2 T. ground cloves
1 T. nutmeg
2 t. ground ginger
zest of 1 orange
Optional: 1 T. vanilla extract
Garnish: orange slices, fresh parsley, kumquats, cranberries

Score surface of ham with a knife and press whole cloves into ham; place in a slow cooker. Pour in cider to cover all except top 2 inches of ham. Pack brown sugar over top of ham, pressing firmly; drizzle with syrup. Sprinkle with spices, zest and vanilla, if using. Add remaining cider without going over fill line. Cover and cook on low setting for 8 to 10 hours. Garnish before serving. Serves 12.

Claire Bertram
Lexington, KY

Rosemary + Thyme Chicken

3-lb. roasting chicken
1 to 2 T. garlic, minced
kosher salt to taste
½ onion, sliced into wedges
4 sprigs fresh rosemary

3 sprigs fresh thyme
seasoning salt to taste
Garnish: lemon wedges, fresh
rosemary, fresh thyme

"My family loves this recipe...I use fresh herbs from my garden."

—Linda

Rub inside of chicken with garlic and kosher salt. Stuff with onion and herb sprigs. Sprinkle seasoning salt on the outside of chicken; place in a slow cooker. Cover and cook on low setting for 8 to 10 hours. Garnish with lemon wedges, rosemary and thyme. Serves 4.

Linda Sather
Corvallis, OR

Orange-Glazed Cornish Hens

A very special dinner for two!

make it easy

The key to making orange zest is to do it with a light touch. Use a zester or a very fine grater so that you get fine pieces of skin. Avoid the white pith beneath the skin, as it is bitter.

2 20-oz. Cornish game hens, thawed
salt and pepper to taste
8-oz. pkg. chicken-flavored stuffing mix, prepared
1 c. chicken broth
1 orange, sliced
¼ t. orange zest
¼ c. orange juice
2 T. honey
1 T. lemon juice
1½ t. oil
Garnish: oranges, fresh sage

Sprinkle hens inside and out with salt and pepper. Spoon prepared stuffing loosely into hens and truss closed. Place hens neck-end down in a large slow cooker. Stir together remaining ingredients except garnish in a bowl; pour over hens. Cover and cook on low setting for 5 to 7 hours, basting once or twice with sauce in slow cooker, until juices run clear when hens are pierced. Spoon sauce over hens to serve. Garnish with whole and sliced oranges and sprigs of fresh sage. Serves 2.

Jo Ann
Gooseberry Patch

Herb-Roasted Turkey

A new way to prepare tender, delicious turkey...guests will love it!

5 to 6-lb. turkey breast
¼ c. water
¼ c. cream cheese, softened
2 T. butter, softened
1 T. soy sauce
1 green onion, finely chopped
1 clove garlic, finely chopped
1 T. fresh parsley, minced
½ t. dried basil
½ t. dried thyme
½ t. poultry seasoning
¼ t. pepper

Place turkey breast-side up in a slow cooker; add water. Blend together remaining ingredients in a small bowl; spread over outside of turkey. Cover and cook on low setting for 8 to 10 hours or on high setting for 4 to 6 hours. Serves 6 to 8.

Tori Willis
Champaign, IL

Bacon + Sage Roast Turkey

The easiest-ever Thanksgiving dinner...all you need to add is cranberry sauce and dessert!

slow-cooker secrets

When a slow-cooker roast recipe gives a range of cooking times such as 8 to 10 hours, roasts will be tender after 8 hours and can be sliced neatly. After 10 hours, they will shred... perfect for sandwiches with sauce.

8 new redskin potatoes, halved
1½ c. baby carrots
½ t. garlic-pepper seasoning
6-lb. turkey breast
12-oz. jar roast turkey gravy
2 T. all-purpose flour

4 to 6 slices bacon, crisply cooked and crumbled
1 T. Worcestershire sauce
¾ t. dried sage
Garnish: fresh sage

Arrange potatoes and carrots in a slow cooker; sprinkle with seasoning. Place turkey breast-side up on top of vegetables. Combine gravy, flour, bacon, Worcestershire sauce and sage in a small bowl. Mix well and pour over turkey and vegetables. Cover and cook on low setting for 7 to 9 hours, until juices run clear when turkey is pierced. Garnish with fresh sprigs of sage. Serves 8.

Jamie Johnson
Gooseberry Patch

No-Fuss Turkey Breast

With only three ingredients, prep time is amazingly fast.

5-lb. turkey breast
1.35-oz. pkg. onion soup mix

16-oz. can whole-berry cranberry sauce

Place turkey breast in a slow cooker. Combine soup mix and cranberry sauce in a bowl; spread over turkey. Cover and cook on low setting for 6 to 8 hours. Serves 6.

Pat Wissler
Harrisburg, PA

Bacon & Sage
Roast Turkey

Kielbasa & Red
Beans, page 84

5 ingredients or less

Nothing's easier than getting these dishes with only five ingredients or less into the slow cooker, ready to simmer until tender. No-Peek Shepherd's Pie is a one-dish meal with only four ingredients. Warm some garlic bread to serve with Italian Sausage & Penne. For a new take on broccoli casserole, enjoy Ham & Broccoli Meal-in-One. These recipes are simply delicious!

Teriyaki Beef

Teriyaki Beef

⅓ c. teriyaki marinade
8-oz. can crushed pineapple, undrained

1½-lb. boneless beef chuck steak
Optional: hot cooked noodles

Spray a slow cooker with non-stick vegetable spray; add marinade and pineapple. Place steak in marinade mixture. Cover and cook on high setting for 2½ to 3½ hours. Serve over cooked noodles. Serves 4.

Molly Cool
Marysville, OH

"With only three ingredients, this is the recipe I reach for when I find time's short!"

—Molly

Easy Special Pot Roast

10¾-oz. can Cheddar cheese soup
10¾-oz. can golden mushroom soup

10¾-oz. can French onion soup
3-lb. beef chuck roast

Mix soups in a slow cooker; top with roast. Cover and cook on low setting for 8 to 9 hours, turning roast halfway through cooking time if possible. Serves 6.

Marge Dicton
Bartonsville, PA

"This is one of my family's most-requested meals! It's so easy and makes a delicious gravy for egg noodles or potatoes. We like it anytime...it's especially great on cold, snowy winter days!"

—Marge

safe handling

Keep a pair of long, padded oven mitts nearby when slow cooking...they're perfect for lifting and carrying the hot crock safely.

Newlywed Beef & Noodles

> "I got married recently, and this is one of my first original recipes."
>
> —Shannon

1 lb. stew beef cubes, browned
3 14½-oz. cans beef broth
3 to 4 cubes beef bouillon
8-oz. pkg. egg noodles, uncooked

Add beef, broth and 3 broth cans of water to a slow cooker; stir in bouillon cubes. Cover and cook on low setting for 4 to 6 hours; add noodles. Cover and cook on low setting until noodles are done. Serves 4.

Shannon Kennedy
Delaware, OH

Missy's Easy Pork Roast

You won't believe how tender and delicious this roast is! It's wonderful with mashed potatoes.

2 to 3-lb. pork roast
1½-oz. pkg. onion soup mix
¾ to 1 c. milk
2 slices bacon, halved

Place roast in a slow cooker; set aside. Combine soup mix and milk in a bowl and spread over roast. Lay bacon slices on top of roast. Cover and cook on low setting for 6 to 8 hours. Serves 4 to 6.

Missy Frost
Xenia, OH

simple side

Try a new side dish instead of rice or noodles…barley pilaf. Simply prepare quick-cooking barley with chicken broth, seasoned with a little chopped onion and dried parsley. Quick, tasty and filling!

Easy Round Steak
Ashley Whitehead (Sidney, TX)

Like lots of gravy? Use two packages of soup mix and two cans of soup.

2 to 2½-lb. beef round steak
1½-oz. pkg. onion soup mix
¼ c. water

10¾-oz. can cream of mushroom soup

Slice steak into 5 serving-size pieces; place in a slow cooker. Add soup mix, water and soup; cover and cook on low setting for 6 to 8 hours. Serves 5.

Lone Star
Barbecue Ribs

Lone Star Barbecue Ribs

Use the barbecue sauce of your choice, such as hickory or mesquite flavor.

3 lbs. bone-in beef short ribs
1 c. water
½ c. barbecue sauce

½ c. dry red wine or beef broth
1 T. Worcestershire sauce

Arrange ribs in a slow cooker. Mix together remaining ingredients in a bowl and pour over ribs. Cover and cook on low setting for 8 to 10 hours. Serves 4 to 6.

Gail Galipp
Mabank, TX

No-Peek Shepherd's Pie

1 lb. ground pork sausage, browned and drained
10-oz. pkg. frozen peas and carrots

24-oz. pkg. prepared mashed potatoes
12-oz. jar beef gravy

Combine sausage with peas and carrots in a slow cooker. Spoon mashed potatoes evenly over mixture; top with gravy. Do not stir. Cover and cook on low setting for 4 to 6 hours. Serves 6.

Melanie Lowe
Dover, DE

"We love this filling one-dish meal! Sometimes I'll use ground beef instead of sausage...it's good either way. Just add some brown & serve rolls and dinner is served."

—Melanie

Italian Sausage + Penne

Pop some garlic bread in the oven…dinner is ready!

¾ lb. hot Italian sausage links, cut into bite-size pieces
1 red pepper, chopped
½ onion, chopped
26-oz. jar spaghetti sauce
8-oz. pkg. penne pasta, cooked

Stir together all ingredients except pasta in a slow cooker. Cover and cook on low setting for 7 to 8 hours. At serving time, stir in cooked pasta. Serves 4.

Nancy Stizza-Ortega
Oklahoma City, OK

flavor tip

For a little less heat, use sweet turkey Italian sausage links instead of hot.

Kielbasa + Red Beans

Serve over bowls of rice for traditional red beans & rice.

1 lb. Kielbasa sausage, cut into bite-size pieces
4 to 5 16-oz. cans kidney beans, drained and rinsed
2 14½-oz. cans diced tomatoes, undrained
1 onion, chopped
hot pepper sauce to taste

Combine all ingredients in a slow cooker. Cover and cook on low setting for 8 hours or on high setting for 4 to 5 hours. Serves 6 to 8.

Beth Schlieper
Lakewood, CO

autumn evening picnic

A hearty dish like Italian Sausage & Penne or Kielbasa & Red Beans is perfect on a cool autumn evening. Carry the crock right out to your backyard picnic table and savor the fall colors with your family!

Italian Sausage
& Penne

Ham & Broccoli Meal-in-One

Hope Davenport (Portland, TX)

This main-dish rice cooks up while you are away...a truly trouble-free meal!

3 c. cooked long-cooking rice
2 16-oz. pkgs. frozen chopped
   broccoli, thawed
16-oz. jar pasteurized process
   cheese sauce

2 10¾-oz. cans cream of chicken
   soup
salt and pepper to taste
1 lb. cooked ham cubes

Combine all ingredients except ham in a slow cooker. Cover and cook on low setting for 3½ hours. Add ham and mix well. Cover and cook on low setting for 15 to 30 more minutes. Serves 6 to 8.

Brown Sugar Ham

With only a few ingredients, you can create the most amazing flavor for this boneless ham.

½ c. brown sugar, packed
1 t. dry mustard
1 t. prepared horseradish

¼ c. cola, divided
5 to 6-lb. boneless smoked ham, halved

Combine brown sugar, mustard, horseradish and 2 tablespoons cola in a bowl; mix well. Rub over ham; place in a slow cooker. Drizzle remaining cola over ham. Cover and cook on low setting for 8 to 10 hours, until a meat thermometer inserted in thickest part of ham reads 140 degrees. Serves 15 to 20.

Melanie Lowe
Dover, DE

Pineapple Chicken

Very simple…very good!

6 boneless, skinless chicken breasts
salt, pepper and paprika to taste

20-oz. can pineapple tidbits, drained
2 T. Dijon mustard

Arrange chicken in a slow cooker; sprinkle with salt, pepper and paprika. Set aside. Mix together pineapple and mustard in a bowl; spread over chicken. Cover and cook on high setting for 3 to 4 hours. Serves 6.

Tonya Lewis
Crothersville, IN

slow-cooker secrets

Allow a little extra time when slow-cooking in the summer…high humidity can cause food to take longer to finish cooking.

Fiesta Chicken Pronto

"This is delicious served over rice! We like to shred the chicken and use it for tacos and burritos, too."

—Kristi

8 boneless, skinless chicken breasts
16-oz. can black beans, drained and rinsed
10¾-oz. can cream of chicken soup
2 T. taco seasoning mix
¼ c. salsa

Arrange chicken in a slow cooker. Combine remaining ingredients in a bowl and pour over chicken. Cover and cook on high setting for 3 hours. Serves 8.

Kristi Duis
Maple Plain, MN

Zesty Picante Chicken

Spice up suppertime with yummy southwestern-style chicken breasts…made in the slow cooker!

"We like to double the recipe and just roll up the leftovers in tortillas…tomorrow's dinner is ready."

—Sonya

4 boneless, skinless chicken breasts
16-oz. jar picante sauce
15½-oz. can black beans, drained and rinsed
4 slices American cheese
2¼ c. cooked rice
Optional: green onions, chopped

Place chicken in a 5-quart slow cooker; add picante sauce. Spread black beans over the top. Cover and cook on high setting for 3 hours, or until juices run clear when chicken is pierced. Top with cheese slices; cover and heat until melted. Spoon over rice to serve. Garnish with green onions, if desired. Serves 4.

Sonya Collett
Sioux City, IA

Zesty Picante
Chicken

Zesty Italian Chicken

Not your usual chicken dinner!

slow-cooker secrets

Quartered potatoes or tiny, tender new potatoes can simply be placed on top of the chicken…they'll steam to perfection while the chicken slow-cooks.

4 boneless, skinless chicken breasts
½ c. Italian salad dressing, divided
½ c. grated Parmesan cheese, divided
1 t. Italian seasoning, divided
4 potatoes, quartered

Arrange chicken in a slow cooker; sprinkle with half each of salad dressing, Parmesan cheese and Italian seasoning. Add potatoes; top with remaining dressing, Parmesan cheese and seasoning. Cover and cook on low setting for 8 hours or on high setting for 4 hours. Serves 4.

Alice Ardaugh
Joliet, IL

Nacho Chicken + Rice

Make wraps by spooning into flour tortillas, folding over and rolling up from the bottom.

1 lb. boneless, skinless chicken breasts, cubed

2 10¾-oz. cans Cheddar cheese soup

16-oz. jar chunky salsa

1¼ c. water

1¼ c. uncooked long-cooking rice

Combine all ingredients in a slow cooker. Cover and cook on low setting for about 5 hours, or until chicken and rice are tender. Serves 6 to 8.

Candace Whitelock
Seaford, DE

Chicken + Cornbread

You can add a drained can of green beans to the stuffing mix for a real all-in-one meal!

4 boneless, skinless chicken breasts

10¾-oz. can cream of mushroom soup

6-oz. pkg. cornbread stuffing mix

½ c. water

Place chicken in a slow cooker and set aside. Mix together remaining ingredients in a bowl; pour over chicken. Cover and cook on low setting for 6 to 8 hours. Serves 4.

Cynthia Stimson
Lake City, FL

make it easy

Change flavors by simply substituting a different cooking liquid. Try your favorite creamy soup, or replace water with seasoned broth or whatever you have on hand... just be sure to add the same amount.

Chicken Swiss Supreme

slow-cooker secrets

If there seems to be a bit too much liquid inside the slow cooker, and it's almost dinnertime, tilt the lid and turn the slow cooker to the high setting...soon the liquid will begin to evaporate.

3 slices bacon, crisply cooked, crumbled and drippings reserved
6 boneless, skinless chicken breasts
4-oz. can sliced mushrooms, drained
10¾-oz. can cream of chicken soup
½ c. Swiss cheese, diced

Cook chicken in reserved bacon drippings in a skillet over medium heat for 3 to 5 minutes, until lightly golden, turning once. Place chicken in a slow cooker; top with mushrooms. Add soup to skillet; heat through and pour over chicken. Cover and cook on low setting for 4 to 5 hours, until juices run clear when chicken is pierced. Top chicken with cheese and sprinkle with bacon. Increase heat to high setting. Cover and cook for 10 to 15 minutes, until cheese is melted. Serves 6.

Lynn Williams
Muncie, IN

Creamy Chicken & Noodles

3 to 4 boneless, skinless
chicken breasts
2 10¾-oz. cans cream of
chicken soup

½ c. butter, sliced
4 10½-oz. cans chicken broth
24-oz. pkg. frozen egg noodles
Garnish: fresh parsley

"We've shared this recipe with many other families...they love it, too!"

—Melissa

Combine all ingredients except noodles and garnish in a slow cooker. Cover and cook on low setting for 8 hours. One hour before serving, remove chicken, shred and return to slow cooker. Stir in frozen noodles; cover and cook on low setting for one hour. Serve in soup bowls. Garnish with parsley. Serves 4 to 6.

Melissa Dennis
Marysville, OH

Autumn Supper Chicken

With just a few ingredients, this is ready for the slow cooker in no time...go jump in the fall leaves!

4 boneless, skinless chicken breasts
1¼-oz. pkg. taco seasoning mix

1 c. salsa
¼ c. sour cream
tortillas or cooked rice

Place chicken breasts in a lightly greased slow cooker; sprinkle seasoning mix over chicken. Top with salsa; cover and cook on low setting for 8 hours. Remove chicken to a plate; shred and set aside. Add sour cream to salsa mixture; stir in chicken. Serve with tortillas or over cooked rice. Serves 4.

Debbie Byrne
Clinton, CT

"A delicious recipe from my grandma!"

—Elisha

Barbecue Chicken

4 boneless, skinless chicken breasts
1 c. barbecue sauce

¾ c. chicken broth
1 sweet onion, sliced
salt and pepper to taste

Place all ingredients in a slow cooker; stir gently. Cover and cook on low setting for 6 to 7 hours or on high setting for 3 hours. Serves 4.

Elisha Wiggins
Suwanee, GA

Stuffed Game Hens

If you like a crispier skin, just place hens under the broiler for a few minutes.

2 20-oz. Cornish game hens,
   thawed
salt and pepper to taste

8-oz. pkg. chicken-flavored
   stuffing mix, prepared

Sprinkle hens all over with salt and pepper; stuff loosely with prepared stuffing. Wrap each hen tightly in a length of aluminum foil; arrange in slow cooker. Spoon any extra stuffing onto a length of foil and make a sealed packet; place on top of hens. Cover and cook on low setting for 6 to 8 hours, until juices run clear when hens are pierced. Serves 2.

Lisa Bownas
Columbus, OH

make it easy

A quick go-with for a slow-cooker meal...toss steamed green beans, broccoli or zucchini with a little olive oil and chopped fresh herbs.

Beef Enchiladas,
page 98

melting pot
flavorful meals from all over

Take a flavor trip around the world! Beef Enchiladas transport you south of the border. Swedish Cabbage Rolls, packed with meat and rice, are truly comfort food. You'll find that Chinese-Style Barbecue Pork and Orange Teriyaki Chicken are easier to make than picking up take-out for dinner!

Beef Enchiladas

Cheesy and easy! Serve with tortilla chips.

make it easy

Rinsing canned beans gets rid of the thick liquid in the can and reduces the sodium by 40 percent.

1 lb. ground beef, browned and drained
15½-oz. can pinto beans, drained and rinsed
15-oz. can corn, drained
10¾-oz. can cream of mushroom soup
10¾-oz. can nacho cheese soup
10-oz. can enchilada sauce
½ c. onion, chopped
½ c. sliced black olives
4 corn tortillas
2 c. shredded Cheddar cheese, divided
Optional: shredded lettuce, chopped tomato

Combine all ingredients except tortillas, shredded cheese, lettuce and tomato in a large bowl. Place one tortilla in the bottom of a slow cooker; spoon one-fourth of the beef mixture over tortilla, followed by ½ cup cheese. Repeat layers until all ingredients are used, ending with cheese. Cover and cook on high setting for one hour, or until cheese is melted and bubbling. Top with lettuce and tomato, if desired. Serves 6 to 8.

Laura Harp
Bolivar, MO

Carne Guisada

Serve this hearty Mexican stew with warm tortillas, guacamole and shredded cheese…also great with cornbread and greens!

2 lbs. beef rump roast, trimmed and cubed
salt and pepper to taste
2 lbs. potatoes, peeled and chopped
10¾-oz. can cream of mushroom with roasted garlic soup
4-oz. can chopped green chiles
1 t. ground cumin

Sprinkle beef cubes with salt and pepper. Combine with remaining ingredients in a slow cooker. Cover and cook on low setting for 8 to 10 hours. If desired, mash lightly with a potato masher after cooking. Serves 6.

Deborah Sheffield
Huntsville, TX

Cantonese Dinner

This recipe is a family favorite. Whether served over rice or chow mein noodles, it's full of flavor!

1½ to 2 lbs. boneless beef round steak, cut into strips
1 T. oil
1 onion, chopped
1 green pepper, chopped
12 oz. sliced mushrooms

8-oz. can tomato sauce
3 T. brown sugar, packed
1½ T. vinegar
2 t. Worcestershire sauce
1½ t. salt

Brown beef strips in oil in a skillet over medium heat; drain. Place beef, onion, green pepper and mushrooms in a slow cooker. Combine remaining ingredients in a small bowl and mix well; pour over meat and vegetables. Cover and cook on low setting for 6 to 8 hours or on high setting for 3 hours. Serves 4.

Lisa Ludwig
Fort Wayne, IN

make it faster

To cut down on prep time, purchase prechopped onion and green pepper and presliced mushrooms, which you'll find in most grocery produce departments. They are real time-savers.

Beef Goulash

"This family favorite was not originally created for the slow cooker, but when it became popular and my mother went back to work, she adapted her recipe for the new 'gadget.'"

—Wendy

2 lbs. stew beef cubes
¼ c. oil
2 28-oz. cans potatoes, drained and rinsed
4 carrots, peeled and sliced
8-oz. can tomato sauce
3 c. water

1 clove garlic, minced
1 T. paprika
1 t. dried marjoram
1 t. lemon zest
½ t. salt
2 cubes beef bouillon

Brown beef in oil in a medium skillet over medium-high heat. Combine beef and remaining ingredients in a slow cooker. Cover and cook on low setting for 7 hours or on high setting for 4 hours. Serves 4 to 5.

Wendy Paffenroth
Pine Island, NY

German Sauerbraten

Serve with spaetzle noodles tossed with butter and topped with chopped fresh parsley.

4 to 5-lb. beef rump roast
2 t. salt
1 t. ground ginger
2½ c. water
2 c. cider vinegar
2 onions, sliced
⅓ c. sugar

2 T. pickling spice
1 t. whole peppercorns
8 whole cloves
2 bay leaves
2 T. oil
16 to 20 gingersnaps, crushed

make it easy

Garden-fresh herbs are delicious…if you have them on hand, just use double the amount of dried herbs called for in a recipe.

Rub roast all over with salt and ginger; place in a deep glass bowl and set aside. Combine water, vinegar, onions, sugar and spices in a saucepan; bring to a boil. Pour over roast; turn to coat. Cover roast and refrigerate for 3 days, turning twice each day. Remove roast, reserving marinade; pat dry. Heat oil in a Dutch oven; brown roast on all sides. Place roast in a slow cooker. Strain marinade, reserving half of onions and spices. Pour 1½ cups marinade, onions and spices over roast; refrigerate remaining marinade. Cover and cook on low setting for 6 to 7 hours, until roast is tender. Remove roast to a platter; keep warm. Discard onions and spices; add enough of refrigerated marinade to liquid from slow cooker to equal 3½ cups. Pour into a saucepan; bring to a boil. Add crushed gingersnaps; simmer until gravy thickens. Slice roast; serve with gravy. Serves 12 to 14.

Lenore Mincher
Patchogue, NY

Company Beef Bourguignonne

This dish is good enough to serve to guests! Sprinkle extra crumbled bacon over each portion, if you like.

slow-cooker secrets

Add tender fresh veggies such as mushrooms and zucchini near the end of cooking time…they'll stay firm and brightly colored.

3 lbs. boneless beef round steak, cubed
6 slices bacon, crisply cooked and crumbled, drippings reserved
1 onion, sliced
1 c. baby carrots
salt and pepper to taste
3 T. all-purpose flour
10½-oz. can beef broth
1 T. tomato paste

2 cloves garlic, minced
½ t. dried thyme
1 bay leaf
16-oz. pkg. sliced mushrooms
1 T. oil
15-oz. jar pearl onions, drained
½ c. Burgundy wine or beef broth
Garnish: fresh thyme

Brown beef cubes in reserved bacon drippings in a skillet over medium-high heat; place in a slow cooker. Add onion, carrots, salt and pepper to skillet; stir in flour. Add broth and tomato paste; mix well and pour over beef. Sprinkle bacon, garlic and herbs over beef. Cover and cook on low setting for 8 to 10 hours. One hour before serving, sauté mushrooms in oil in skillet over medium-high heat; add to slow cooker along with pearl onions and wine or broth. Discard bay leaf. Garnish with thyme. Serves 4 to 6.

Melanie Lowe
Dover, DE

Braciola Stuffed Beef

If you've never tried this, you don't know what you're missing!

2 lbs. boneless beef round
  steak
½ c. seasoned dry bread
  crumbs
½ c. grated Parmesan cheese
1 T. garlic, minced
1 egg, beaten

¼ t. pepper
2 eggs, hard-boiled, peeled and
  minced
32-oz. jar meatless spaghetti
  sauce, divided
hot cooked linguine pasta

Place steak between 2 lengths of wax paper; pound until thin and set
aside. Mix together bread crumbs, cheese, garlic, egg, pepper and sieved
eggs in a bowl; spread over steak. Roll up steak and tie at one-inch inter-
vals with kitchen string. Spread one cup spaghetti sauce in the bottom of a
slow cooker; set a rack on top. Place rolled-up steak on rack; cover with
remaining sauce. Cover and cook on low setting for 6 to 8 hours, until steak
is very tender. Slice between strings and serve over hot linguine. Serves 6.

Joan Brochu
Hardwick, VT

Russian Beef Borscht

Serve in big soup bowls, dollop with sour cream and garnish with fresh dill sprigs…there's nothing better on a cold day!

slow-cooker secrets

Easy does it! Scrub the crockery liner gently…a nylon scrubbie is just right for removing cooked-on food particles.

4 c. cabbage, thinly sliced
1½ lbs. beets, peeled and grated
5 carrots, peeled and sliced
1 parsnip, peeled and sliced
1 c. onion, chopped
1 lb. stew beef cubes

4 cloves garlic, minced
14½-oz. can diced tomatoes
3 14½-oz. cans beef broth
¼ c. lemon juice
1 T. sugar
1 t. pepper

Layer ingredients in a slow cooker in order given. Cover and cook on low setting for 7 to 9 hours, just until vegetables are tender. Serves 8 to 10.

Rita Morgan
Pueblo, CO

Swedish Cabbage Rolls

Comfort food…just like Mom used to make.

12 large leaves cabbage
1 egg, beaten
¼ c. milk
¼ c. onion, finely chopped
1 t. salt
¼ t. pepper
½ lb. ground beef

½ lb. ground pork
1 c. cooked rice
8-oz. can tomato sauce
1 T. brown sugar, packed
1 T. lemon juice
1 t. Worcestershire sauce
Garnish: sour cream

Immerse cabbage leaves in a large saucepan of boiling water for about 3 minutes, or until limp; drain well and set aside. Combine egg, milk, onion, salt, pepper, beef, pork and cooked rice in a bowl; mix well. Place about ¼ cup meat mixture in the center of each cabbage leaf; fold in sides and roll ends over meat. Arrange cabbage rolls in a slow cooker. Combine remaining ingredients except garnish in a small bowl and pour over rolls. Cover and cook on low setting for 7 to 9 hours. Spoon sauce over rolls and garnish with sour cream. Serves 6.

Linda Sinclair
Valencia, CA

lazy day quick fix

A rainy day cure-all…toss together all the ingredients for a tasty slow-cooker meal, make some popcorn and enjoy a classic movie marathon. When you're ready for dinner, it's ready for you!

Dutch Spareribs & Dumplings

Dumplings are stick-to-your-ribs fall fare!

slow-cooker secrets

Drop the dumpling dough onto the simmering sauerkraut rather than directly into the liquid. The dumplings will steam rather than settle into the liquid and become soggy.

3 lbs. country-style pork
  spareribs
29-oz. can sauerkraut, drained
  and rinsed
2 tart apples, peeled, cored and
  cut into wedges

1 c. onion, chopped
2 t. seasoned salt
½ t. seasoned pepper
¼ t. caraway seed

Slice spareribs into serving portions and trim any excess fat; place in a lightly greased slow cooker. Top ribs with sauerkraut, apples and onion; sprinkle with seasonings. Cover and cook on low setting for 8 hours, or until ribs are very tender when pierced. Remove excess liquid above sauerkraut with a bulb baster. Drop Dumplings by heaping tablespoonfuls on top of sauerkraut. Cover and cook on high setting for 30 minutes, or until dumplings are fluffy. Serves 4 to 6.

Dumplings:

2 c. all-purpose flour
2 t. baking powder
1 t. salt

½ t. caraway seed
1 egg
¾ c. milk

Combine flour, baking powder and salt in a large bowl; stir in caraway seed. Beat egg in a cup with a fork; beat in milk. Pour all at once into flour mixture; stir until blended.

Sharon Crider
Lebanon, MO

Chinese-Style Barbecue Pork

2-lb. boneless pork roast
¼ c. soy sauce
¼ c. hoisin sauce
3 T. catsup
3 T. honey
2 t. garlic, minced
2 t. fresh ginger, peeled and
  grated

1 t. dark sesame oil
½ t. Chinese 5-spice powder
½ c. chicken broth
cooked rice
Garnish: green onions,
  chopped

make it easy

It's always best to fluff rice with a fork after cooking instead of stirring with a spoon…with a fork it's sure to be fluffy every time!

Place roast in a large plastic zipping bag and set aside. Whisk together remaining ingredients except broth, rice and garnish; pour over roast. Seal bag; refrigerate at least 2 hours, turning occasionally. Place roast in a slow cooker; pour marinade from bag over roast. Cover and cook on low setting for 8 hours. Remove pork from slow cooker; keep warm. Add broth to liquid in slow cooker; cover and cook on low setting for 30 minutes, or until thickened. Shred pork with 2 forks and stir into sauce in slow cooker. Serve over cooked rice; garnish with chopped green onions. Serves 6.

Ruth Leonard
Columbus, OH

Southwestern
Pork Chalupas

Southwestern Pork Chalupas

16-oz. pkg. dried pinto beans
4 c. water
4-oz. can chopped green chiles
2 T. chili powder
2 t. ground cumin
1 t. dried oregano
salt and pepper to taste
4-lb. pork shoulder roast
16-oz. pkg. corn chips
Garnish: shredded Mexican-blend cheese, sour cream, salsa, fresh cilantro

Cover beans with water in a large saucepan; soak overnight. Drain. Combine beans, 4 cups water, chiles and seasonings in a slow cooker. Add roast; cover and cook on low setting for 4 hours. Remove roast and shred, discarding bones; return pork to slow cooker. Cover and cook on low setting for 2 to 4 more hours, adding more water if necessary. Arrange corn chips on serving plates; top with pork mixture. Garnish as desired. Serves 8.

Vickie
Gooseberry Patch

make it faster

For a speedier start, simply use two to three 15-ounce cans of pinto beans.

Barbecue Pulled-Pork Fajitas

2½-lb. boneless pork loin roast, trimmed
1 onion, thinly sliced
2 c. barbecue sauce
¾ c. chunky salsa, hot or mild
1 T. chili powder
1 t. ground cumin
16-oz. pkg. frozen stir-fry peppers and onions
½ t. salt
18 8 to 10-inch flour tortillas, warmed
Toppings: sour cream, shredded Mexican-blend cheese, guacamole

Place roast in a slow cooker; top with onion. Mix sauce, salsa, chili powder and cumin in a bowl; pour over roast. Cover and cook on low setting for 8 to 10 hours. Remove roast and shred, using 2 forks. Return to slow cooker and mix well; add stir-fry vegetables and salt. Increase heat to high setting; cover and cook for 30 more minutes. Fill each tortilla with ½ cup pork mixture and desired toppings. Serves 12 to 18.

Jackie Valvardi
Haddon Heights, NJ

"We like to spice up these slow-cooker fajitas with shredded Pepper Jack cheese, guacamole and sour cream."

—Jackie

Jammin' Jambalaya

Yum! This feeds a crowd...and everybody loves it.

1 lb. boneless, skinless
   chicken breasts, cubed
1 lb. andouille sausage, sliced
28-oz. can diced tomatoes,
   undrained
1 onion, chopped
1 green pepper, chopped
1 c. celery, chopped
1 c. chicken broth

2 t. Cajun seasoning
2 t. dried oregano
2 t. dried parsley
1 t. cayenne pepper
½ t. dried thyme
1 lb. frozen cooked shrimp,
   thawed and tails removed
cooked rice

Place chicken, sausage, tomatoes, onion, pepper, celery and broth in a slow cooker. Stir in seasonings; mix well. Cover and cook on low setting for 7 to 8 hours or on high setting for 3 to 4 hours. Add shrimp during final 30 minutes of cooking time. Serve over cooked rice. Serves 10 to 12.

Valarie Dennard
Palatka, FL

Arroz con Pollo

¼ t. saffron
2 T. boiling water
3 lbs. boneless, skinless
　chicken breasts
1 T. oil
2 onions, finely chopped
4 cloves garlic, minced
1 t. salt
¼ t. pepper
1½ c. long-cooking rice,
　uncooked

28-oz. can whole tomatoes,
　chopped
1 c. chicken broth
½ c. dry white wine or
　chicken broth
1 green pepper, finely chopped
1 c. frozen green peas, thawed
Garnish: sliced green olives
　with pimentos
Optional: hot pepper sauce

make it faster

Keep frozen chopped onions, peppers and veggie blends on hand for quick slow-cooker meal prep. They'll thaw quickly, so you can assemble a recipe in a snap...no peeling, chopping or dicing!

Combine saffron and boiling water in a cup; set aside. Cook chicken in oil in a skillet over medium-high heat just until golden. Place chicken in a slow cooker and set aside. Add onions to skillet. Reduce heat to medium; cook and stir until softened. Add garlic, salt and pepper; cook and stir for one minute. Add rice; cook and stir until coated. Add saffron mixture, tomatoes, broth and wine or broth; pour over chicken. Cover and cook on low setting for 6 to 8 hours, until juices run clear when chicken is pierced and rice is tender. Increase heat to high setting; add green pepper and peas. Cover and cook 20 more minutes. Garnish with olives; serve with hot sauce, if desired. Serves 6.

Michelle Sheridan
Huntsville, AL

a Caribbean favorite

Arroz con pollo simply means rice with chicken. It's a traditional dish of Latin America and Spain and is considered a classic favorite in several Caribbean countries. The chicken in this one-pot meal is infused with the flavors of the vegetables as it simmers.

French Country Chicken

> "This recipe is completely my own, and we really love it! It has sophisticated flavors, yet takes only minutes to prepare. The white wine really makes this dish, but you can use chicken broth instead."
>
> —Teri

1 onion, chopped
6 carrots, sliced diagonally
6 stalks celery, sliced diagonally
6 boneless, skinless chicken breasts
1 t. dried tarragon
1 t. dried thyme
pepper to taste
10¾-oz. can cream of chicken soup
1½-oz. pkg. onion soup mix
⅓ c. dry white wine or chicken broth
2 T. cornstarch
cooked rice

Combine onion, carrots and celery in the bottom of a slow cooker. Arrange chicken on top; sprinkle with seasonings. Combine chicken soup and onion soup mix in a bowl; spoon over chicken. Cover and cook on high setting for 4 hours, stirring after one hour. At serving time, stir together wine or broth and cornstarch in a small bowl; pour over chicken and mix well. Cook, uncovered, for 10 more minutes, or until thickened. Stir again; serve over rice. Serves 6.

Teri Lindquist
Gurnee, IL

Coq Au Vin

4 boneless, skinless chicken breasts
16-oz. pkg. sliced mushrooms
15-oz. jar pearl onions, drained
½ c. dry white wine or chicken broth
1 t. dried thyme
1 bay leaf
1 c. chicken broth
⅓ c. all-purpose flour
cooked rice
2 t. fresh parsley, chopped

Place chicken in a slow cooker; top with mushrooms and onions. Drizzle with wine or broth and sprinkle thyme over top; add bay leaf. Stir together broth and flour in a small bowl; pour into slow cooker. Cover and cook on low setting for 5 hours, or until juices run clear when chicken is pierced. Discard bay leaf. Serve over rice; sprinkle with parsley. Serves 4.

Kendall Hale
Lynn, MA

Italian Chicken

The spaghetti sauce mix is the secret flavoring in this quick-to-fix dinner.

1 t. garlic powder
1 t. seasoned salt
1 t. pepper
3 lbs. chicken, skin removed
1 T. oil
1.37-oz. pkg. spaghetti sauce mix

1½ t. Italian seasoning
1 c. dry white wine or chicken broth
4 c. zucchini, sliced ½-inch thick
Optional: hot cooked thin spaghetti

Mix garlic powder, seasoned salt and pepper in a cup; rub chicken with mixture. Heat oil in a large skillet over medium heat; brown chicken on all sides, about 2 minutes. Combine chicken, sauce mix, Italian seasoning and wine or broth in a slow cooker. Cover and cook on low setting for 7 to 8 hours or on high setting for 3 to 4 hours. Add zucchini during last hour of cooking and cook on low setting. Serve over hot cooked spaghetti, if desired. Serves 6.

Nola Coons
Gooseberry Patch

My Brother's Seafood Paella

*"My brother,
who does all the
cooking for his family,
shared this delicious
recipe with me."*

—Pamela

1 c. long-cooking rice,
  uncooked
2 c. water
1 onion, diced
14½-oz. can diced tomatoes,
  undrained
3 cloves garlic, minced
1 t. salt
1 t. pepper

⅛ t. saffron
Optional: ¼ t. cayenne pepper
½ lb. mild fish fillets, cut into
  1-inch cubes
½ lb. scallops
½ lb. uncooked medium
  shrimp, peeled and cleaned
8-oz. pkg. frozen peas, thawed
Garnish: lemon wedges

Combine rice, water, onion, tomatoes, garlic and seasonings in a slow
cooker; mix thoroughly. Cover and cook on high setting for 2 to 3 hours.
Add fish, scallops, shrimp and peas; cover and cook on high setting for one
more hour. Serve with lemon wedges. Serves 4.

Pamela Barry
Huntington, IN

Orange Teriyaki Chicken

Who would guess that the secret ingredient is orange marmalade?

1½ c. chicken broth
½ c. teriyaki sauce
½ c. green onions, sliced and divided
3 cloves garlic, minced
¾ c. orange marmalade

2 T. cornstarch
8 boneless, skinless chicken thighs
cooked rice
½ c. walnuts, coarsely chopped

Mix broth, sauce, ¼ cup green onions, garlic, marmalade and cornstarch in a slow cooker. Add chicken; turn to coat. Cover and cook on low setting for 8 to 9 hours. Serve over rice; garnish with walnuts and remaining green onions. Serves 4 to 6.

Tina Goodpasture
Meadowview, VA

slow-cooker secrets

A slow cooker is oh-so handy, but don't use it to reheat cooked foods…it just doesn't warm up quickly enough. Instead, simmer on the stovetop or place in the microwave for a few minutes, until bubbly.

Savory Low-Country Shrimp + Grits

Paired with a fresh spinach salad, this is a favorite meal...and using a slow cooker makes it easy to prepare, even on a busy day.

6 c. chicken broth
¾ t. salt
1½ c. quick-cooking grits, uncooked
1 green pepper, chopped
½ c. red pepper, chopped
6 green onions, chopped
2 cloves garlic, chopped
1½ lbs. uncooked small shrimp, peeled and cleaned

2 T. butter
1½ c. shredded sharp Cheddar cheese
1½ c. shredded Monterey Jack cheese
2 10-oz. cans diced tomatoes with green chiles, drained
Optional: ¼ t. cayenne pepper, chopped green onions, chopped fresh parsley

Place broth, salt and grits in an ungreased slow cooker; cover and cook on low setting for 6 to 8 hours. Two hours before serving, sauté peppers, onions, garlic and shrimp in butter in a skillet over medium-high heat about 5 minutes, or until vegetables are tender and shrimp are pink. Add vegetable mixture, cheeses, tomatoes and cayenne pepper, if using, to slow cooker. Turn to high setting; cover and cook 2 more hours. Garnish with green onions and parsley, if desired. Serves 4 to 6.

Sharon Candler
Villa Rica, GA

shrimp...fresh or frozen?

Unsure which shrimp to buy? Fresh shrimp is highly perishable and should be eaten within 24 hours of purchase. While thawed shrimp should be kept only a couple of days, shrimp stored in the freezer will keep for several weeks. Thaw frozen shrimp in the refrigerator or in ice-cold water and allow to drain before using.

Mom's Firehouse Chili, page 120

chilis, chowders, soups + stews

Here's a bounty of warming soups and stews. Whether you prefer your chili mild, spicy, beefy or with chicken, we have options to please your tastes. Late autumn vegetables make a potful of Farmers' Market Stew. Buffalo Chicken Wing Soup combines the ingredients of a favorite appetizer into the heartiness of a favorite soup! Which one of these recipes will be your new favorite?

Krysti's Delicious Chili

Serve chili with a variety of toppings such as crackers, sour cream and chopped green onions.

1 lb. ground beef, browned and drained
2 28-oz. cans crushed tomatoes
2 15-oz. cans light red kidney beans
3 T. dried, minced onion
1 T. chili powder
1 T. sugar or to taste
salt and pepper to taste
Garnish: shredded Cheddar cheese, chopped fresh parsley

Place all ingredients except garnish in an ungreased 4-quart slow cooker. Cover and cook on high setting for 4 hours. Garnish with cheese and parsley. Serves 6.

Krysti Hilfiger
Covington, PA

Mom's Firehouse Chili

1½ lbs. boneless beef chuck roast, cubed
3 onions, sliced
2 c. water
28-oz. can crushed tomatoes
6-oz. can tomato paste
2 stalks celery, sliced
16-oz. can kidney beans, drained and rinsed
16-oz. can cannellini beans, drained and rinsed
1 green pepper, cut into strips
pepper, garlic powder, dried parsley, chili powder and hot pepper sauce to taste
14¾-oz. can corn, drained
Garnish: sour cream, shredded Cheddar cheese, chopped green onions

Place beef, onions, water, tomatoes and tomato paste in a slow cooker; stir well. Add celery, beans and green pepper. Stir in seasonings to taste; top with corn. Cover and cook on low setting for 8 to 10 hours or on high setting for 5 to 6 hours, stirring occasionally. Garnish as desired. Serves 6.

Wendy Lee Paffenroth
Pine Island, NY

Krysti's Delicious Chili

Kathleen's Fabulous Chili

"This recipe is my own creation. It won first place for 'Overall Best Chili' at a church chili cook-off!"

—Kathy

1 lb. ground beef
½ to 1 lb. bacon, chopped
1 onion, chopped
½ green pepper, diced
2 15½-oz. cans dark red kidney beans, drained and rinsed
15½-oz. can light red kidney beans, drained and rinsed
15½-oz. can pinto beans

16-oz. can pork & beans
15½-oz. can Sloppy Joe sauce
14½-oz. can diced tomatoes, drained and juice reserved
¼ to ½ c. brown sugar, packed
salt, pepper and chili powder to taste
Garnish: sour cream, sliced green onions, shredded Cheddar cheese

Brown ground beef and bacon with onion and green pepper in a skillet over medium heat; drain. Combine all ingredients except garnish in a slow cooker, using half of reserved tomato juice; cover and cook on high setting until chili just begins to simmer, about one hour. Reduce heat to low setting; continue to simmer, covered, for 2 to 4 hours. Add remaining tomato juice if more liquid is needed. Garnish as desired. Serves 6 to 8.

Kathy Murray Strunk
Mesa, AZ

Smoky White Bean Chili

5 15½-oz. cans Great Northern
  beans, drained and rinsed
16-oz. pkg. mini smoked
  sausages
10-oz. can diced tomatoes
  with green chiles

1 T. dried, minced onion
1 T. chili powder
salt and pepper to taste

Combine all ingredients in a slow cooker. Cover and cook on low setting for about 4 hours. Serves 6 to 8.

Lorrie Smith
Drummonds, TN

"I love white bean chili but don't care for the chicken, so I decided to try it with smoked sausages. Now I wouldn't make it any other way!"

—Lorrie

Elizabeth's White Chili

Garnish with crushed white-corn tortilla chips ... a clever use for those broken chips that linger at the bottom of the bag!

make it faster

A fun new way to serve cornbread...mix up the batter, thin slightly with a little extra milk and then bake until crisp in a waffle iron. Perfect with your favorite soup or chili!

1 lb. boneless, skinless chicken breasts, cooked and shredded
4 15½-oz. cans Great Northern beans, undrained
16-oz. jar salsa
8-oz. pkg. shredded Pepper Jack cheese
2 t. ground cumin
½ c. chicken broth
Optional: 12-oz. can beer or 1½ c. chicken broth

Combine all ingredients except optional beer or broth in a 5-quart slow cooker. Add beer or broth for a thinner consistency, if desired. Cover and cook on low setting for 4 hours, or until heated through. Serves 6 to 8.

Elizabeth Tipton
Knoxville, TN

Jalapeño Chicken Chili

Lisa Case (Clovis, CA)

2 c. chicken, cooked and cubed
4 15.8-oz. cans Great Northern
  beans
1 onion, chopped
½ c. red pepper, diced
½ c. green pepper, diced
2 jalapeño peppers, seeded and
  finely diced

2 cloves garlic, minced
1½ t. ground cumin
¾ t. salt
½ t. dried oregano
½ t. chicken bouillon granules
¼ c. water
1 to 2 c. salsa
Optional: tortilla chips

Combine all ingredients except salsa and chips in a slow cooker. Cover and cook on low setting for 8 to 10 hours or on high setting for 5 hours. Add salsa during last hour of cooking. Before serving, stir well to blend. Serve with tortilla chips. Serves 8.

Bacon-Corn Chowder

Ideal for toting to a harvest bonfire supper.

5 c. redskin potatoes, cubed
16-oz. pkg. frozen corn
6 slices bacon, crisply cooked
  and crumbled
¼ c. dried, minced onion
2 14½-oz. cans chicken broth
1 c. water
2 t. garlic salt

1 t. pepper
¼ t. turmeric
12-oz. can evaporated milk
8-oz. pkg. shredded Monterey
  Jack cheese
Optional: fresh chives,
  chopped

    Combine all ingredients except milk, cheese and chives in a slow cooker. Cover and cook on low setting for 8 to 9 hours, until potatoes are tender. Stir in milk and cheese; cover and cook until cheese melts. Garnish with chives, if desired. Serves 4 to 6.

Linda Keehn
Chatham, IL

Chow-Down Corn Chowder

6 slices bacon, diced
½ c. onion, chopped
2 c. potatoes, peeled and diced
2 10-oz. pkgs. frozen corn
16-oz. can creamed corn

1 T. sugar
1½ t. Worcestershire sauce
1¼ t. seasoned salt
½ t. pepper
1 c. water

"So easy to prepare with a slow cooker. It's delicious!"

—Marian

Fry bacon in a skillet over medium heat until crisp. Remove bacon; reserve drippings. Add onion and potatoes to drippings and sauté over medium-high heat 5 minutes; drain well. Combine all ingredients in a slow cooker; stir well. Cover and cook on low setting for 4 to 6 hours. Serves 4.

Marian Buckley
Fontana, CA

New England Clam Chowder

Once you taste this, you'll never go back to canned chowder!

½ c. butter, melted
2 T. onion powder
2 t. dried thyme
2 stalks celery, chopped
46-oz. can clam juice
2 cubes chicken bouillon
2 bay leaves
3 16-oz. cans whole potatoes, drained and diced
3 10-oz. cans whole baby clams, undrained
2 c. light cream
2 c. milk
salt and pepper to taste

Stir together butter, onion powder, thyme and celery in a slow cooker; cover and cook on high setting for 30 minutes. Add clam juice, bouillon, bay leaves and potatoes. Cover and continue cooking on high setting for 2 hours. Add clams; reduce heat to low setting. Cover and cook for 2 more hours. Stir in cream and milk; cover and cook one more hour, or until heated through. Before serving, discard bay leaves; add salt and pepper to taste. Serves 6.

Virginia Watson
Scranton, PA

serve it up

A collection of coffee mugs is fun for serving soup! Pick up one-of-a-kind novelty or souvenir mugs for a song at yard sales.

Divine Seafood Chowder

This chowder is a meal all by itself!

1 onion, sliced
4 potatoes, peeled and sliced
minced garlic to taste
1 t. dill weed
2 T. butter
1 c. clam juice, heated to
  boiling
15-oz. can creamed corn

salt and pepper to taste
½-lb. haddock or cod fillet
½ lb. uncooked medium
  shrimp, peeled, cleaned and
  halved
1 c. light cream, warmed
Optional: fresh dill, chopped

Layer all ingredients except cream and dill in a slow cooker, placing fish and shrimp on top. Cover and cook on high setting for one hour; reduce heat to low setting and cook for 3 hours. Add cream; stir gently and serve. Garnish with chopped fresh dill, if desired. Serves 4 to 6.

Audrey Laudenat
East Haddam, CT

Souped-Up Clam Chowder

"We love crunchy oyster crackers with this creamy chowder."

—Cheri

3 10¾-oz. cans clam chowder
2 10¾-oz. cans cream of celery soup
10¾-oz. can cream of onion soup
2 6½-oz. cans minced clams
4 c. half-and-half
½ c. butter

Combine all ingredients in a slow cooker; cover and cook on low setting for 6 hours. Serves 10 to 12.

Cheri Emery
Quincy, IL

Sausage-Bean Chowder

The perfect meal for a cozy weekend at home.

1 lb. ground pork sausage
1 onion, chopped
32-oz. can Great Northern beans, drained and rinsed
16-oz. can chopped tomatoes, undrained
1 potato, chopped
2 c. water
½ t. dried basil

Brown sausage and onion together in a large skillet over medium-high heat; drain. Place sausage and onion in a 4-quart slow cooker and add remaining ingredients; stir. Cover and cook on low setting for 5 to 6 hours. Serves 6.

Nancy Hines
Flushing, MI

Down-on-the-Bayou Gumbo

You can't help but smile with a bowl of gumbo right in front of you! Using a slow cooker means it's ready when you get home.

3 T. all-purpose flour
3 T. oil
3 c. chicken broth
½ lb. smoked pork sausage, sliced
2 c. frozen okra
14½-oz. can diced tomatoes
1 onion, chopped
1 green pepper, chopped
3 cloves garlic, minced
¼ t. cayenne pepper
¾ lb. cooked medium shrimp, tails removed
cooked rice
Garnish: chopped fresh parsley

Stir together flour and oil in a saucepan over medium heat. Cook, stirring constantly, for 5 minutes. Reduce heat to low; cook and stir for 10 minutes, or until mixture is reddish brown. Pour broth into a slow cooker; stir in flour mixture. Add remaining ingredients except shrimp, rice and parsley. Cover and cook on low setting for 7 to 9 hours. Add shrimp to slow cooker; mix well. Cover and cook on low setting for 30 minutes. Ladle gumbo over cooked rice in bowls. Garnish with chopped parsley. Serves 6.

Sue Nealy
Greenville, IL

Steak Soup

2½-lb. beef sirloin tip roast, cut into 1-inch cubes
¼ c. all-purpose flour
½ t. salt
½ t. pepper
2 T. canola oil
1-oz. pkg. onion soup mix
4 c. beef broth
1 T. tomato paste
1 T. Worcestershire sauce
2 c. uncooked wide egg noodles

Combine beef, flour, salt and pepper in a large plastic zipping bag; seal bag and shake to coat beef. Sauté beef in hot oil in a Dutch oven over medium-high heat 6 minutes, or until browned. Place in a slow cooker. Sprinkle soup mix over beef. Whisk together broth, tomato paste and Worcestershire sauce in a bowl; pour over beef. Cover and cook on low setting for 8 hours, or until beef is tender. Add noodles to slow cooker; cover and cook 30 minutes, or until noodles are done. Serves 6.

Midwestern Steakhouse Soup

If the potatoes haven't thickened the broth as much as you'd like, simply whisk 2 tablespoons cornstarch into ¼ cup cold water and then stir into the soup and cook a little longer.

1½ lbs. boneless beef top sirloin steak, about ½-inch thick, sliced into thin strips
2 T. oil
1 sweet onion, sliced
8-oz. pkg. sliced mushrooms
3 14½-oz. cans beef broth
4 c. water
3 potatoes, cut into ½-inch cubes
2 t. Worcestershire sauce
Garnish: 8-oz. pkg. shredded Monterey Jack cheese, chopped fresh parsley

Brown steak strips in oil in a Dutch oven over medium heat for 5 minutes. Add onion and mushrooms; sauté until tender, about 5 to 10 minutes. Add remaining ingredients except garnish; simmer over low heat for 30 to 40 minutes. Transfer to a slow cooker. Cover and cook on low setting for up to 4 hours. Ladle into bowls and serve garnished with cheese and chopped parsley. Serves 6 to 8.

Barbara Cooper
Orion, IL

Buffalo Chicken Wing Soup

Buffalo Chicken Wing Soup

This spicy, creamy soup warms you up from your toes to your nose on a cold winter day!

6 c. milk
3 10¾-oz. cans cream of chicken soup
3 c. chicken, cooked and shredded
1 c. sour cream
¼ to ½ c. hot pepper sauce
Garnish: shredded Monterey Jack cheese, chopped green onions, hot pepper sauce

Combine all ingredients except garnish in a 5-quart slow cooker. Cover and cook on low setting for 4 to 5 hours. To serve, garnish with cheese, green onions and additional hot pepper sauce. Serves 8.

Anna McMaster
Portland, OR

Hamburger Soup

It's wonderful to come home and find this scrumptious soup waiting for you!

1 lb. ground beef, browned and drained
28-oz. can crushed tomatoes
1 c. potatoes, peeled and diced
1 c. carrots, peeled and chopped
1 c. onion, sliced
1 c. celery, sliced
4 c. hot water
1 T. salt
½ t. pepper
½ t. dried basil
½ t. dried thyme
1 bay leaf, crumbled

Mix together all ingredients in a slow cooker. Cover and cook on low setting for 6 to 8 hours, until vegetables are tender. Serves 4 to 6.

Barbara Pache
Marshall, WI

South-of-the-Border Chicken Soup

Black beans and salsa add a Mexican flair to this filling soup that's a snap to make in the slow cooker.

> "The ladies at church like this recipe because it's healthy and best of all...easy!"
>
> —Paula

2 to 3 boneless, skinless chicken breasts
15-oz. can black beans, drained and rinsed
15¼-oz. can corn, drained
24-oz. jar salsa
tortilla chips
Optional: sour cream, shredded Cheddar cheese

Layer chicken, beans, corn and salsa in a slow cooker. Cover and cook on low setting for 6 to 8 hours, until juices run clear when chicken is pierced. Using 2 forks, shred chicken and return to slow cooker; ladle soup into bowls. Serve with chips and top with desired toppings. Serves 6 to 8.

Paula Lee
Lapel, IN

Chile Verde Soup
Lisa Sett (Thousand Oaks, CA)

½-lb. pork tenderloin, cut into
½-inch cubes

1 t. oil

2 c. chicken broth

2 15-oz. cans cannellini or Great
Northern beans, drained and
rinsed

2 4-oz. cans diced green chiles

¼ t. ground cumin

¼ t. dried oregano

salt and pepper to taste

Optional: fresh cilantro, chopped

Cook pork in oil in a skillet over medium heat for one to 2 minutes, until browned. Place pork in a slow cooker. Add remaining ingredients except cilantro; stir well. Cover and cook on low setting for 4 to 6 hours. Sprinkle cilantro over each serving, if desired. Serves 6 to 8.

Bacon & Wild Rice Soup

"This smells great when I come home after a long day of work or shopping!"

—Judy

1 lb. bacon, crisply cooked and crumbled
1 c. celery, chopped
1 onion, diced
12-oz. pkg. sliced mushrooms
1 c. cooked instant wild rice
2 10¾-oz. cans cream of mushroom soup
2 10¾-oz. cans cream of chicken soup
2 c. water
2 c. half-and-half

Combine all ingredients except half-and-half in a slow cooker. Cover and cook on low setting for 8 to 10 hours or on high setting for 4 to 6 hours. Stir in half-and-half 30 minutes before end of cooking time. Serves 8.

Judy Sellgren
Wyoming, MI

Turkey & Wild Rice Soup

This hearty soup is chock-full of veggies! Make it even healthier by using fat-free broth and evaporated milk, if you wish.

2 t. oil
½ c. onion, chopped
1 c. deli smoked turkey, diced
1 c. celery, diced
1 c. carrots, peeled and diced
½ c. long-cooking wild rice, uncooked

1 t. dried tarragon
¼ t. pepper
2 4-oz. cans chicken broth
12-oz. can evaporated milk
⅓ c. all-purpose flour
1 c. frozen peas, thawed
Optional: 2 T. dry sherry

Heat oil in a skillet over medium heat. Add onion and cook for about 4 minutes, or until tender, stirring occasionally. Combine onion, turkey, celery, carrots, rice, tarragon and pepper in a slow cooker; stir in broth. Cover and cook on low setting for 6 to 8 hours, until vegetables and rice are tender. Mix evaporated milk and flour in a small bowl; stir into soup along with peas and sherry, if using. Cover again and cook on low setting for about 20 minutes, or until thickened. Serves 6.

Judith Jennings
Ironwood, MI

Kielbasa Soup

This is a terrific cold-weather soup…warms you right up after a hockey game!

1½ to 2 lbs. Kielbasa sausage, thinly sliced
4 qts. water
16-oz. pkg. frozen mixed vegetables

6-oz. can tomato paste
1 onion, chopped
3 potatoes, diced
Optional: chopped fresh parsley

Combine all ingredients except parsley in a slow cooker. Cover and cook on low setting for 10 to 12 hours. Garnish individual servings with parsley, if desired. Serves 8.

make it easy

When freezing soup, leave a little headspace at the top… it needs room to expand as it freezes.

French Onion Soup

This soup makes a large volume and freezes well if not eaten all at once.

6 large sweet onions, thinly sliced
¼ c. butter, melted
½ t. salt
½ t. pepper
32-oz. container beef broth
2 10½-oz. cans beef consommé

¼ c. dry white wine
1 t. fresh thyme leaves
8 to 10 ½-inch thick French bread baguette slices
½ c. Gruyère cheese, shredded
Garnish: fresh thyme

Combine onions, butter, salt and pepper in a lightly greased slow cooker. Cover and cook on low setting for 8 hours. Stir broth, consommé, wine and one teaspoon thyme into onion mixture. Cover and cook 15 more minutes, or until hot. Meanwhile, sprinkle baguette slices with cheese; place on a lightly greased baking sheet. Broil 3 inches from the heat for one to 2 minutes, until cheese melts. Serve soup with cheese toasts. Garnish with thyme. Serves 8 to 10.

make it healthy

Cutting down on salt? Choose lower-sodium broth, canned soups and veggies. You can also use garlic powder instead of garlic salt…just taste and adjust the seasonings when food has finished cooking.

Old-Fashioned Bean Soup

16-oz. pkg. dried navy beans
2 qts. water
1 meaty ham bone
1 onion, chopped
½ c. celery leaves, chopped
5 peppercorns
salt to taste
Optional: bay leaf

Cover beans with water in a Dutch oven; soak overnight. Drain. Combine beans, 2 quarts water and remaining ingredients in a slow cooker. Cover and cook on low setting for 10 to 12 hours or on high setting for 5 to 6 hours. Remove ham bone; dice meat and return to slow cooker. Discard bay leaf, if using. Serves 8 to 10.

Kathleen Poritz
Burlington, WI

"I'm a teacher's aide with outdoor winter recess duty...brrr! So I freeze any extra bean soup in small containers to take for lunch. It really warms up the body and soul."

—Kathleen

Vegetable-Beef Soup

1 lb. ground beef, browned
  and drained
16-oz. pkg. frozen mixed
  vegetables
12-oz. can cocktail vegetable
  juice
3 c. water
½ c. pearled barley
1½-oz. pkg. onion soup mix
3 cubes beef bouillon

Combine all ingredients in a slow cooker. Cover and cook on low setting for 6 to 8 hours. Serves 4 to 6.

Cami Cherryholmes
Urbana, IA

"This recipe is as good-tasting as it is easy...it also freezes well!"

—Cami

Easy Potato Soup

4 to 5 potatoes, peeled and
  cubed
10¾-oz. can cream of celery
  soup
10¾-oz. can cream of chicken
  soup
1⅓ c. water

4⅔ c. milk
6.6-oz. pkg. instant mashed
  potato flakes
Optional: bacon bits, chopped
  green onions, shredded
  Cheddar cheese

Place potatoes, soups and water in a 5-quart slow cooker. Cover and cook on high setting for 2 to 3 hours, until potatoes are tender. Add milk and instant mashed potato flakes to reach desired consistency, stirring constantly. Cover and cook for 2 to 3 more hours; spoon into bowls to serve. Top with bacon bits, green onions and Cheddar cheese, if desired. Serves 4 to 6.

Easy Beef Stew

"My sister, Crystal, gave me this wonderful recipe. It's so yummy and easy. All you need is fruit and warm bread to make a meal!"

—Christy

1½ lbs. stew beef cubes
8-oz. pkg. baby carrots
3 to 4 potatoes, cubed
10¾-oz. can tomato soup

10¾-oz. can French onion
  soup
10¾-oz. can beef broth

Place beef in bottom of a slow cooker sprayed with non-stick vegetable spray. Arrange carrots and potatoes over beef. Combine soups and broth in a bowl; pour over vegetables. Cover and cook on low setting for 8 to 10 hours or on high setting for 4 hours. Serves 3 to 4.

Christy Neubert
O'Fallon, IL

Farmers' Market Stew

½ lb. stew beef cubes
2 ½-inch thick boneless pork chops, cubed
1 T. olive oil
2 carrots, chopped
2 parsnips, peeled and chopped
2 potatoes, peeled and chopped
1 stalk celery, chopped
2 apples, peeled, cored and cut into 1-inch cubes
2 T. quick-cooking tapioca, uncooked
1 c. apple cider
1 c. water
2 t. beef bouillon granules
Optional: ½ c. red wine
¼ t. pepper
¼ t. dried thyme
¼ t. dried rosemary
salt to taste
Garnish: fresh rosemary, fresh thyme

slow-cooker secrets

Stir in a little quick-cooking tapioca with other ingredients for a stew or roast...the broth will thicken magically as it cooks!

Brown beef and pork in oil in a large skillet over medium heat; drain. Place vegetables and apples in a slow cooker; sprinkle with tapioca. Add beef and pork. Combine remaining ingredients except salt and garnish in a small bowl; pour over beef and pork. Cover and cook on low setting for 8 to 10 hours or on high setting for 4 to 6 hours. Add salt to taste before serving. Garnish with rosemary and thyme. Serves 6.

Verona Haught
Londonderry, NH

Stroganoff Stew

1½ lbs. stew beef cubes
2 T. butter
3 to 4 potatoes, peeled and cubed
2 to 3 carrots, peeled and sliced
½ c. celery, chopped
1 onion, chopped
½ t. salt-free tomato-basil garlic seasoning
¼ t. dried thyme
¼ t. pepper
⅛ t. salt
10¾-oz. can cream of mushroom soup
1½ c. water
8-oz. container sour cream

Place beef and butter in a large skillet. Cook over medium heat until beef is browned; set aside. Arrange potatoes, carrots, celery and onion in a slow cooker. Sprinkle with seasonings. Stir in beef. Cover and cook on low setting for 8 hours. Combine soup, water and sour cream in a bowl; spoon over beef mixture in slow cooker. Stir to blend. Serves 4.

Jackie Everson
Bangor, WI

Nancy's Winter Stew

10¾-oz. can tomato soup
¼ c. dry red wine or beef broth
1⅓ c. water
½ c. onion, chopped
¼ t. Italian seasoning
salt and pepper to taste
2 to 3 potatoes, peeled and cubed
2 carrots, peeled and sliced ½-inch thick
14½-oz. can green beans, drained
1 doz. frozen meatballs

Mix together soup, wine or broth and water in a slow cooker. Stir in remaining ingredients. Cover and cook on low setting for 8 to 9 hours. Serves 4.

Nancy Fagan
Warminster, PA

Homestyle Chicken Stew

Jennifer Oglesby (Brownsville, IN)

1 lb. boneless, skinless chicken
  breasts, cubed
2 c. potatoes, peeled and cubed
1 stalk celery, sliced
2 carrots, peeled and sliced
14½-oz. can chicken broth

6-oz. can tomato paste
½ t. paprika
¼ t. pepper
¼ t. dried thyme
1½ T. cold water
1 T. cornstarch

Combine all ingredients except water and cornstarch in a slow cooker. Mix together well. Cover and cook on low setting for 7 to 8 hours or on high setting for 3½ hours. About 30 minutes before serving time, stir together water and cornstarch in a small bowl and stir into stew. Cover and cook on high setting for 30 more minutes, or until thickened. Serves 4.

Easy Brunswick Stew

Make preparation a breeze by stopping at your local supermarket deli or favorite barbecue restaurant for shredded pork.

3 lbs. shredded cooked pork
4 c. water
4 c. frozen diced potatoes
3 14½-oz. cans diced tomatoes with garlic and onion

14½-oz. can corn, drained
14½-oz. can creamed corn
2 c. frozen lima beans
½ c. barbecue sauce
1 T. hot pepper sauce
1 t. pepper

Stir together all ingredients in a slow cooker. Cover and cook on high setting for 4 hours. Serves 10 to 12.

slow-cooker secrets

For quick clean-up, add a disposable slow-cooker liner before adding ingredients, or give the inside of the cooker a good coating of non-stick vegetable spray.

Autumn Stew

"One evening I made a campfire bundle out of chicken and vegetables. It was so good that I thought I would try it in the slow cooker with turkey, sweet potatoes, potatoes and squash... it turned out even better!"

—Rachel

2 butternut squash, peeled and diced
4 potatoes, peeled and quartered
2 sweet potatoes, peeled and diced
2 c. buttermilk

14½-oz. can beef broth
½ t. cinnamon
⅛ t. ground cloves
28-oz. can turkey, drained
1 t. dried parsley
½ t. dried sage
¼ c. cornstarch

Arrange squash and potatoes in a slow cooker; pour in buttermilk and beef broth. Sprinkle vegetables with cinnamon and cloves. Add turkey; sprinkle with parsley and sage. Cover and cook on high setting for 5 hours, or until potatoes are tender. Whisk in cornstarch and cook until sauce thickens. Serves 8 to 10.

Rachel Boyd
Defiance, OH

Santa Fe Turkey Stew — Michele Dochat (Lititz, PA)

2 16-oz. cans pinto beans
2 16-oz. cans navy beans
2 16-oz. cans black beans
2 16-oz. cans kidney beans
3 lbs. cooked turkey, cubed
3 49½-oz. cans chicken broth
2 to 3 6-oz. pkgs. frozen shoepeg corn

2 28-oz. cans diced tomatoes
1 c. onion, diced
4 to 5 stalks celery, diced
3 1-oz. pkgs. ranch salad dressing mix
1¼-oz. pkg. taco seasoning mix
salt and pepper to taste

Drain and rinse all beans; combine with remaining ingredients in a 6½-quart slow cooker. Cover and cook on low setting for 8 to 10 hours or on high setting for 4 hours. Serves 10 to 12.

Southern-Style Pulled
Pork Sandwiches,
page 159

sandwiches + more

Layer up the meat to create favorite sandwiches for any occasion. Heartland Barbecued Beef becomes tender when simmered in the slow cooker. Homestyle Sloppy Joes satisfy the hungry appetite. Southwestern flavors are featured in Mexican Roll-Ups and Mexicali Beef Soft Tacos. Pile up the pitas and tacos with all of the fixin's for an anytime lunch or supper.

Heartland Barbecued Beef

So much flavor for so little effort.

2-lb. beef chuck roast, cut
   crosswise into ¼-inch slices
½ c. onion, chopped
2 cloves garlic, minced
2 c. catsup
¼ c. brown sugar, packed

¼ c. Worcestershire sauce
1 t. mustard
½ t. salt
¼ t. pepper
6 to 8 onion buns, split

Combine all ingredients except buns in a slow cooker; mix well. Cover and cook on low setting for 6 to 8 hours, stirring occasionally, until meat is tender. Serve on buns. Serves 6 to 8.

Sharon Crider
Junction City, KS

Virginia-Style Beef Sandwiches

Add a side of coleslaw or potato salad, and you have the makings for a picnic!

2½ to 3-lb beef round or
   shoulder roast
1 c. catsup
12-oz. can beer or
   non-alcoholic beer

1½-oz. pkg. onion soup mix
8 sandwich buns, split
Garnish: bottled barbecue
   sauce

Place roast in a slow cooker; set aside. Mix together catsup, beer and soup mix in a bowl; pour over roast. Cover and cook on low setting for 4 to 4½ hours. Shred roast with 2 forks. Spoon shredded beef onto buns and serve topped with barbecue sauce. Serves 8.

Ursula Juarez-Wall
Dumfries, VA

make it easy

Juicy BBQ sandwiches are best served on a vintage-style oilcloth…saucy spills wipe right up! Look for one with a colorful design of fruit or flowers.

Barbecue Steak Sandwiches

A great party recipe! Roll up leftovers in tortillas for a fast lunch.

3 lbs. boneless beef round steak, cut into several large pieces
2 onions, chopped
¾ c. celery, thinly sliced
½ c. catsup
½ to ¾ c. water
⅓ c. lemon juice
⅓ c. Worcestershire sauce
3 T. brown sugar, packed
3 T. cider vinegar
2 t. mustard
2 t. salt
1 t. pepper
1 t. chili powder
½ t. paprika
½ t. hot pepper sauce
12 to 14 sandwich buns, split

Place meat, onions and celery in a slow cooker; set aside. Combine remaining ingredients except buns in a bowl. Stir and pour over meat. Cover and cook on low setting for 6 to 8 hours, until meat is tender. Remove meat and cool slightly; shred with a fork and return to sauce in slow cooker. Heat through and serve on buns. Serves 12 to 14.

Lisa Sanders
Shoals, IN

warming buns made easy

Warm sandwich buns for a crowd…easy! Fill a roaster with buns, cover with heavy-duty aluminum foil and cut several slits in the foil. Top with several dampened paper towels and tightly cover with more foil. Place in a 250-degree oven for 20 minutes. Rolls will be hot and steamy.

French Dip Sandwiches

Feel free to substitute smaller rolls to make bite-size sandwiches, if desired.

3½ to 4-lb. **boneless beef chuck roast**, trimmed and cut in half

½ c. **soy sauce**

1 cube **beef bouillon**

1 **bay leaf**

3 to 4 **peppercorns**, crushed

1 t. **dried rosemary**, crushed

1 t. **dried thyme**

1 t. **garlic powder**

12 **French sandwich rolls**, split

Place roast in a slow cooker. Combine soy sauce and remaining ingredients except rolls in a small bowl; pour over roast. Add water to slow cooker until roast is almost covered. Cover and cook on low setting for 7 hours, or until meat is very tender. Remove roast, reserving broth and discarding bay leaf; shred roast with 2 forks. Divide shredded meat evenly among rolls; serve with broth for dipping. Serves 12.

Zesty Italian Hoagies

3 to 4-lb. beef rump roast
8-oz. bottle Italian salad
   dressing
12-oz. jar pepperoncini,
   drained
8 hoagie buns, split

Place roast in a slow cooker. Pour salad dressing over roast and arrange pepperoncini on top. Cover and cook on low setting for 8 to 10 hours. Remove roast from slow cooker and shred with a fork. Return to slow cooker; mix with pepperoncini and spoon onto buns. Serves 8.

Patti Davis
Kiowa, OK

"We enjoy these sandwiches at a local Italian restaurant... I think my recipe is just as good!"

—Patti

Hearty Italian Sandwiches

Messy but delicious...pass the napkins, please!

1 lb. ground beef
1 lb. ground Italian pork
   sausage
1 onion, chopped
1 green pepper, chopped
1 red pepper, chopped
1 t. salt
1 t. pepper
½ t. red pepper flakes
¾ c. Italian salad dressing
12 sandwich rolls, split
12 slices provolone cheese

Brown ground beef and sausage together in a skillet over medium-high heat; drain and set aside. Place one-third of onion and peppers in a slow cooker; top with half of meat mixture. Repeat layers with remaining vegetables and meat. Sprinkle with salt, pepper and red pepper flakes; pour salad dressing over top. Cover and cook on low setting for 6 hours. Serve on rolls, topped with cheese. Serves 12.

Kristie Rigo
Friedens, PA

Italian Meatball Subs

"This recipe is so good! I like to make a double batch and freeze half for another meal...the meatballs are good over pasta, too!"

—Clydia

1 lb. ground beef
1 c. Italian-flavored dry bread crumbs
½ c. grated Parmesan cheese
1 T. fresh parsley, minced
1 clove garlic, minced
½ c. milk

1 egg
1½ t. salt
½ t. pepper
8 hoagie or hot dog buns, split
Garnish: grated Parmesan cheese

Combine all ingredients except buns and garnish in a large bowl; mix well. Form into 2-inch balls and place in a slow cooker; pour Sauce over top. Cover and cook on low setting for 8 to 10 hours or on high setting for 4 to 6 hours. To serve, place 3 to 4 meatballs on a bun; top with sauce from slow cooker. Garnish with Parmesan cheese, if desired. Serves 8.

Sauce:

28-oz. can tomato purée
28-oz. can Italian-style crushed tomatoes
½ c. grated Parmesan cheese

2 1½-oz. pkgs. spaghetti sauce mix
salt and pepper to taste

Mix all ingredients in a saucepan; bring to a boil. Reduce heat and simmer until blended.

Clydia Mims
Effingham, SC

Mexican Roll-Ups

Makes a yummy taco salad, too! Just layer ingredients over shredded lettuce in crisp tostada bowls.

2 lbs. beef flank steak
1¼-oz. pkg. taco seasoning mix
1 T. butter
1 c. red onion, diced
1 c. green chiles, diced
1 T. cider vinegar
16-oz. can refried beans

12 8-inch flour tortillas, warmed
1½ c. shredded Cheddar cheese
2 c. cherry tomatoes, diced
8-oz. container sour cream

Rub flank steak on all sides with taco seasoning; place in a slow cooker coated with butter. Add onion, chiles and vinegar; cover and cook on low setting for 9 hours. Remove beef from slow cooker and shred. Place beef back in slow cooker with cooking juices; stir well. Heat refried beans and tortillas according to package directions. Spread one to 2 tablespoons refried beans down the center of each tortilla. Spoon about ⅓ cup beef mixture over refried beans. Top each with cheese, tomato and sour cream; roll up. Serves 12.

Ali Snow
Boston, MA

Mexicali Beef Soft Tacos

Two meals in one! You can make tacos the first night, then warm the remaining meat with barbecue sauce for sandwiches another night.

make it easy

A basket of warmed flour tortillas is a must-have with fajitas and tacos. Simply wrap tortillas in aluminum foil and pop into a 250-degree oven for about 15 minutes...easy!

½ to 1 c. water
4 to 5-lb. beef chuck roast
½ red onion, chopped
3 cloves garlic, peeled
¼ c. oil
1 T. red pepper flakes
2 t. ground cumin
2 t. dried oregano
1 t. pepper
10 to 12 10-inch corn or flour tortillas, warmed
Garnish: shredded lettuce, chopped onion, chopped tomatoes, sour cream, salsa

Pour water into a slow cooker; add roast and set aside. Combine onion, garlic, oil and seasonings in a blender. Blend until mixed; pour over roast. Cover and cook on high setting for about 7 hours, or until roast is very tender. Shred roast with 2 forks; return to slow cooker. Reduce heat to low setting. Cover and cook for one more hour. Fill tortillas with beef mixture; add toppings as desired. Serves 10 to 12.

Kathy Lowe
Orem, UT

Taco Joes

Try garnishing with a little peach or pineapple salsa...really good!

3 lbs. ground beef, browned and drained
16-oz. can refried beans
10-oz. can enchilada sauce
1¼-oz. pkg. taco seasoning mix
16-oz. jar salsa
25 hot dog buns, split
Garnish: shredded Cheddar cheese, shredded lettuce, chopped tomatoes, sour cream

Place ground beef in a slow cooker. Stir in beans, enchilada sauce, taco seasoning and salsa. Cover and cook on low setting for 4 to 6 hours. To serve, fill each bun with ⅓ cup beef mixture and garnish as desired. Serves 25.

Sherry Cress
Salem, IN

Sloppy Joes

It's great to start this in the morning and have it waiting for you when everyone arrives home hungry at dinnertime.

1½ lbs. ground beef
1 c. onion, chopped
2 cloves garlic, minced
¾ c. catsup
½ c. green pepper, chopped
½ c. celery, chopped
¼ c. water

1 T. brown sugar, packed
2 T. mustard
2 T. vinegar
2 T. Worcestershire sauce
1½ t. chili powder
6 to 8 sandwich buns, toasted
Optional: sliced pickles

Brown beef, onion and garlic in a skillet over medium-high heat; drain and set aside. Combine remaining ingredients except buns and pickles in a slow cooker; stir in beef mixture. Cover; cook on low setting for 6 to 8 hours or on high setting for 3 to 4 hours. Spoon onto buns. Garnish with sliced pickles, if desired. Serves 6 to 8.

Shelley Sparks
Amarillo, TX

Jen's Pulled Pork Sandwiches

Diet cola is used in this recipe because it is less sweet in flavor. There's no right or wrong amount of sauce to use…simply stir in as much as you'd like. You can also add sliced jalapeños, minced garlic or sautéed onion and green peppers.

"A recipe I created, this is now one of my most-requested dishes for picnics!"

—Jennifer

3 to 4-lb. boneless pork loin roast, halved
2-ltr. bottle diet cola
2 28-oz. bottles honey barbecue sauce
8 to 10 sandwich buns, split
Garnish: dill pickle chips

Place roast in a slow cooker; add cola. Cover and cook on high setting for one hour; reduce heat to low setting and cook, fat-side up, for 10 to 12 more hours. Remove roast from slow cooker; remove and discard any fat. Discard cooking liquids; clean and wipe slow cooker. Return roast to slow cooker; add barbecue sauce to taste. Cover and cook on low setting for one more hour, or until heated through. Add more sauce, if desired. Serve on buns with dill pickle chips. Serves 8 to 10.

Jennifer Inacio
Hummelstown, PA

Cranberry-Barbecue Pork Rolls

2 to 3-lb. pork loin or roast
salt and pepper to taste
16-oz. can cranberry sauce
½ c. barbecue sauce

Optional: additional barbecue
  sauce
10 sandwich rolls, split

Trim most of the fat from pork. Sprinkle pork with salt and pepper; place in a slow cooker. Mix together sauces in a bowl and spoon over pork. Cover and cook on low setting for 6 to 8 hours, until pork is very tender. Shred pork in slow cooker with 2 forks; add more barbecue sauce if needed. Cover and cook on low setting for 20 to 30 more minutes. Serve on rolls. Serves 10.

Samantha Place
Wilmington, VT

"Slow-cooking the pork makes it super tender, and it's so easy! We like to use our favorite sweet onion barbecue sauce in this recipe."

—Samantha

Southern-Style Pulled Pork Sandwiches

Serve with the barbecue sauce of your choice. If hosting others, set out spicy, mild and sweet sauces so guests can choose their favorite.

1 T. vegetable oil
3½ to 4-lb. boneless pork
  shoulder roast, netted or tied
10½-oz. can French onion
  soup

1 c. catsup
¼ c. cider vinegar
2 T. brown sugar, packed
12 sandwich rolls, split

Heat oil in a skillet over medium heat. Add roast and brown on all sides; place roast in an ungreased slow cooker and set aside. Combine soup, catsup, vinegar and brown sugar in a bowl and mix well; pour over roast. Cover and cook on low setting for 8 to 10 hours, until roast is fork-tender. Place roast on a platter; discard string and let stand 10 minutes. Shred roast, using 2 forks; return to slow cooker and stir to mix with sauce. Spoon meat and sauce onto rolls. Serves 12.

Tina Goodpasture
Meadowview, VA

"Enjoy this southern-style sandwich like we do...served with cole-slaw and dill pickle chips."

—Tina

Southern Barbecue Sandwiches

Serve this either as a main dish with sides or on sandwich buns with coleslaw for a truly great North Carolina-style meal.

3 to 4-lb. pork loin roast
1 c. cider vinegar
2 T. sugar
1 T. salt
1 T. Worcestershire sauce
½ c. catsup
Optional: hot pepper sauce to taste
6 to 8 sandwich buns

Place roast in a slow cooker. Mix together vinegar, sugar and salt in a small bowl. Pour over roast. Cover and cook on low setting for 10 to 12 hours, until meat pulls away from bones. Remove meat from slow cooker and cool; pull apart and shred. Return meat to slow cooker. Mix 6 to 8 tablespoons cooking liquid with Worcestershire sauce and catsup in a bowl. Pour over meat and add hot pepper sauce to taste, if desired; mix well. Spoon shredded meat and sauce onto buns. Serves 6 to 8.

Cyndi Little
Whitsett, NC

Ham-Stuffed French Rolls

Serve the hot rolls right from the slow cooker.

2 c. cooked ham, finely chopped
½ c. Cheddar cheese, diced
⅓ c. mayonnaise
2 T. green onions, minced
1 t. mustard
1 t. sweet pickle relish
Optional: 2 eggs, hard-boiled, peeled and chopped
Optional: 2 T. black olives, chopped
6 large or 8 small French rolls

Combine all ingredients except rolls in a large bowl; set aside. Cut tops or one end off rolls; scoop out most of soft centers. Fill rolls with ham mixture; replace tops or ends of rolls. Place filled rolls in a slow cooker. Cover and cook on low setting for 2 to 3 hours. Serves 6 to 8.

Barbara Fiecoat
Galena, OH

Apple-Pork Barbecue Sandwiches

5 to 7-lb. pork picnic roast
5 cloves garlic, peeled
1 sweet onion, chopped
2 c. hot & spicy barbecue sauce

1½ c. applesauce
1 t. cinnamon
salt and pepper to taste
10 to 12 kaiser rolls, split

Cut roast into 2 or 3 pieces to fit into slow cooker, if necessary, and place in slow cooker. Top with whole garlic cloves and chopped onion; add water to cover roast. Cover and cook on low setting for 10 to 12 hours, or overnight. When pork is tender and easily shredded, drain and discard cooking liquid. Break roast apart in slow cooker and shred, removing any bones; mash and blend in garlic. Combine barbecue sauce and applesauce in a bowl; toss with pulled pork to coat thoroughly. Sprinkle with cinnamon, salt and pepper. Cover and cook on low setting until warmed through. Serve pork spooned into rolls. Serves 10 to 12.

Lynn Matava
Hebron, MD

easy clean-up

When serving sticky, saucy foods like barbecue sandwiches or chicken wings, set out a basket of rolled-up fingertip towels, moistened with lemon-scented water and warmed briefly in the microwave. Such a thoughtful touch!

California Chicken Tacos

This recipe is great for those days when you know the evening will be hectic!

flavor tip

Sprinkle chicken with taco or fajita seasoning before cooking. What a flavor boost!

1 lb. boneless, skinless chicken breasts
1¼-oz. pkg. taco seasoning mix
16-oz. jar favorite salsa
8 to 10 corn taco shells

Garnish: shredded lettuce, diced tomatoes, diced avocado, sour cream, shredded Cheddar cheese

Combine all ingredients except taco shells and garnish in a large bowl. Cover and cook on low setting for 6 to 8 hours or on high setting for 4 hours. Shred chicken and spoon into taco shells; garnish as desired. Serves 8 to 10.

Dawn Morgan
Glendora, CA

Lemon-Garlic Chicken Tacos

6 boneless, skinless chicken
  breasts
1 to 1½ c. lemon juice or
  chicken broth
5 to 6 cloves garlic, minced

salt and pepper to taste
12 corn taco shells
Garnish: shredded lettuce,
  chopped tomatoes,
  shredded Cheddar cheese

Place chicken in a slow cooker. Cover and cook on low setting for 8 hours; drain. Shred chicken and return to slow cooker; add lemon juice to cover, garlic, salt and pepper. Cover and cook on low setting for 4 to 5 more hours. Serve in taco shells and garnish as desired. Serves 12.

Marion Sundberg
Ramona, CA

make it faster

Use the last few minutes that Lemon-Garlic Chicken Tacos are cooking to whip up a speedy black bean salad. Combine 3 cups drained and rinsed black beans, 1½ cup frozen corn (thawed), 1½ cup salsa and ¾ teaspoon ground cumin or chili powder; stir well.

Savory Chicken Sandwiches

4 boneless, skinless chicken
  breasts
1½-oz. pkg. onion soup mix
¼ t. garlic salt
¼ c. Italian salad dressing

¼ c. water
4 sandwich buns, split
Garnish: lettuce, sliced
  cheese, sour cream or ranch
  salad dressing

Place chicken in a slow cooker; sprinkle with soup mix and garlic salt. Pour dressing and water over chicken. Cover and cook on low setting for 8 to 9 hours. Remove chicken and shred with 2 forks; return to slow cooker. Serve with a slotted spoon on buns; garnish as desired. Serves 4.

Jodi Griggs
Richmond, KY

"We've made these sandwiches lots of times when we had family & friends coming for the day...they're so easy to make ahead. Everyone always asks for seconds or thirds!"

—Jodi

Greek Chicken Pitas

Greek Chicken Pitas

Top with crumbled feta cheese and sliced black olives.

1 onion, diced
3 cloves garlic, minced
1 lb. boneless, skinless
  chicken breasts, cut into
  strips
1 t. lemon-pepper seasoning
½ t. dried oregano
¼ t. allspice
¼ c. plain yogurt

¼ c. sour cream
½ c. cucumber, peeled
  and diced
4 rounds pita bread, halved
  and split
Optional: sliced cucumber,
  sliced red onion, feta
  cheese, fresh oregano

Place onion and garlic in a slow cooker; set aside. Sprinkle chicken with seasonings; place in slow cooker. Cover and cook on high setting for 6 hours. Stir together yogurt, sour cream and cucumber in a small bowl; chill. Fill pita halves with chicken and drizzle with yogurt sauce. Garnish as desired. Serves 4.

Peggy Pelfrey
Fort Riley, KS

make it easy

Pita halves are perfect for slow-cooker sandwich fillings…extra easy for little hands to hold without spills!

Carolina Chicken Pitas

1 onion, chopped
1 lb. boneless, skinless
  chicken thighs
1 t. lemon-pepper seasoning

½ t. dried oregano
½ c. plain yogurt
4 rounds pita bread, halved
  and split

Combine all ingredients except yogurt and pita bread in a slow cooker; mix well. Cover and cook on low setting for 6 to 8 hours. Just before serving, remove chicken from slow cooker and shred with 2 forks. Return shredded chicken to slow cooker; stir in yogurt. Spoon into pita bread. Serves 4.

Sharon Tillman
Hampton, VA

simple side

Serve a Greek version of bruschetta alongside Carolina Chicken Pitas. Grill thick slices of sourdough bread until golden, then brush with olive oil, spread with tomatoes to cover bread and sprinkle to taste with crumbled feta and dried oregano.

Tangy Teriyaki Sandwiches

What a combination of flavors…what a winner!

1½ lbs. skinless turkey thighs
½ c. teriyaki baste and
　glaze sauce
3 T. orange marmalade
¼ t. pepper
4 hoagie buns, split
Garnish: sliced green onions

Combine all ingredients except buns and garnish in a slow cooker; cover and cook on low setting for 9 to 10 hours. Remove turkey from slow cooker and shred meat, discarding bones; return to slow cooker. Increase heat to high setting. Cover and cook for 10 to 15 minutes, until sauce is thickened. Serve on hoagie buns. Garnish with green onions. Serves 4.

Kelly Alderson
Erie, PA

Tex-Mex Chili Dogs

"With green chiles and corn chips in this recipe, regular chili dogs are a thing of the past at our home."

—Stacie

1-lb. pkg. hot dogs
2 15-oz. cans chili without
　beans
10¾-oz. can Cheddar cheese
　soup
4-oz. can chopped green chiles
10 hot dog buns, split
Garnish: chopped onions,
　crushed corn chips,
　shredded Cheddar cheese

Place hot dogs in a slow cooker. Combine chili, soup and green chiles in a large bowl; pour over hot dogs. Cover and cook on low setting for 4 to 5 hours. Serve hot dogs in buns; top with chili mixture and garnish as desired. Serves 10.

Stacie Avner
Delaware, OH

Tex-Mex Chili Dogs

Green Bean Casserole,
page 173

scrumptious sides

Side dishes take center stage with Asparagus & Cheese Hot Dish and Fettuccine Garden-Style. Offer Stadium Beans at your next tailgate for a sure-fire winner. Green Bean Casserole gets updated with a flavorful and super-easy sauce. Plus, slow-cooked Mac & Cheese will become a family favorite for years to come.

Buttery Acorn Squash
Melody Taynor (Everett, WA)

Raisins, cinnamon, brown sugar and nutmeg…a scrumptious recipe for fall.

¾ c. brown sugar, packed
2 t. pumpkin pie spice
2 acorn squash, halved and seeded

¾ c. golden raisins
¼ c. butter, sliced
½ c. water

Combine brown sugar and pie spice in a small bowl; spoon into squash halves. Sprinkle with raisins; dot with butter. Wrap each squash half individually in heavy-duty aluminum foil; seal tightly. Pour water into a slow cooker. Place squash, cut-side up, in slow cooker (packets may be stacked). Cover and cook on high setting for 4 hours, or until squash is tender. Open foil packets carefully to allow steam to escape. Serves 4.

Simmered Autumn Applesauce

The kids will love this recipe! It's perfect for the apples you picked together at the orchard. Let the delicious aroma from your slow cooker fill your kitchen on a crisp fall day.

8 apples, several different
    varieties, peeled, cored and
    cubed
1 c. water

½ c. brown sugar, packed
1 t. cinnamon
½ t. pumpkin pie spice

Add all ingredients to a 3- to 4-quart slow cooker; stir. Cover and cook on low setting for 6 to 8 hours. Mash apples with the back of a spoon; stir again. Let cool slightly before serving. Serves 6.

Jennifer Levy
Warners, NY

Baked Apples

8 Jonathan or Granny Smith
    apples, cored
⅓ c. raisins
⅓ c. chopped nuts
⅓ c. brown sugar, packed

1½ t. apple pie spice
2 T. margarine, sliced
½ c. apple cider
1 T. lemon juice

Remove peel from top one-third of each apple. Mix raisins, nuts and brown sugar in a small bowl; spoon into apples. Arrange apples in a greased slow cooker. Sprinkle with apple pie spice; dot with margarine. Mix cider and lemon juice in a small bowl; drizzle over apples. Cover and cook on low setting for 8 hours. Serves 8.

Eva Jo Hoyle
Mexico, MO

"Delectable as either a side or a dessert! Sometimes I'll even fill the slow cooker late at night so we can enjoy this dish for breakfast."

—Eva Jo

Asparagus + Cheese Hot Dish

Family members will gladly eat their veggies!

slow-cooker secrets

Don't crack the crock! Sudden changes from cold to hot are a no-no. Don't set a hot crockery liner on a cold surface...run only warm, not cold, water into a warm crock.

1½ to 2 lbs. asparagus, trimmed and cut into 1-inch pieces
1 egg, beaten
1 c. saltine cracker crumbs
10¾-oz. can cream of asparagus soup
10¾-oz. can cream of chicken soup
¼ lb. pasteurized process cheese spread, cubed
⅔ c. slivered almonds, toasted

Combine all ingredients in a slow cooker; mix well. Cover and cook on high setting for 3 to 3½ hours, until asparagus is tender. Serves 4 to 6.

Dianna Likens
Powell, OH

Green Bean Casserole

Go beyond the standard "recipe on the can" casserole by substituting Alfredo sauce for cream of mushroom soup and adding water chestnuts, Parmesan cheese and toasted pecans.

2 16-oz. pkgs. frozen French-cut green beans, thawed
10-oz. container refrigerated Alfredo sauce
8-oz. can diced water chestnuts, drained
6-oz. jar sliced mushrooms, drained
1 c. shredded Parmesan cheese
½ t. pepper
6-oz. can French-fried onions, divided
½ c. chopped pecans

Stir together beans, Alfredo sauce, water chestnuts, mushrooms, cheese, pepper and half of the French-fried onions in a large bowl; spoon mixture into a lightly greased slow cooker. Cover and cook on low setting for 4½ hours, or until bubbly. Heat pecans and remaining French-fried onions in a small non-stick skillet over medium-low heat, stirring often, one to 2 minutes, until toasted and fragrant; sprinkle over casserole just before serving. Serves 10.

slow-cooker secrets

Enlist your slow cooker as a handy holiday helper! If there's a turkey in the oven and dishes are simmering on the stove, simply fill up slow cookers with potatoes, dressing and other sides and let 'em cook away on the countertop.

Slow-Simmered Green Beans

Stir in some chopped bacon for a smoky taste.

1½ lbs. green beans, sliced
1 stalk celery, diced
¼ c. onion, chopped
¼ c. margarine, sliced
4 cubes beef bouillon
1 T. sugar
1 t. garlic salt
¼ t. dill seed

Place all ingredients in a slow cooker; stir to mix. Cover and cook on low setting for 3 to 4 hours. Serves 6 to 8.

Cathy Lipchak
Mechanicsville, VA

Dijon-Ginger Carrots

A super-simple, dressed-up carrot recipe…your family will love it!

12 carrots, peeled and sliced
⅓ c. Dijon mustard
½ c. brown sugar, packed
1 t. fresh ginger, peeled and
   minced

½ t. salt
⅛ t. pepper
Garnish: fresh parsley, minced

Combine all ingredients in a slow cooker. Cover and cook on high setting for 2 to 3 hours, until carrots are tender, stirring twice during cooking time. Garnish with parsley. Serves 10 to 12.

Angela Murphy
Tempe, AZ

Stadium Beans

½ lb. bacon
1 onion, chopped
1 to 2 hot peppers, chopped
2 16-oz. cans baked beans,
  drained
16-oz. can kidney beans,
  drained
15½-oz. can chili beans,
  drained

15-oz. can butter beans,
  drained
2 14½-oz. cans green beans,
  drained
⅔ c. catsup
⅓ c. brown sugar, packed
1 t. chili powder
½ t. ground cumin

Cook bacon in a skillet over medium heat until crisp. Drain bacon on paper towels, reserving drippings in skillet; crumble bacon. Add onion and peppers to drippings; sauté until tender. Combine all the beans in a slow cooker; add crumbled bacon, onion mixture and any remaining drippings. Stir together catsup, brown sugar and spices in a bowl; gently fold into bean mixture. Cover and cook on low setting for 3 to 6 hours. The bean mixture may also be placed in a greased 3- to 4-quart casserole dish and baked, covered, at 350 degrees for one hour. Serves 12 to 16.

"I first tasted these beans at a friend's wedding rehearsal dinner. I've been serving them ever since! It's my most-requested recipe, wonderful for covered-dish dinners, picnics and, of course, tailgating."

—Diana

Diana Krol
Nickerson, KS

Collard Greens

Have some cornbread or rolls handy for sopping up the juices. A sprinkling of hot pepper sauce is the ultimate Southern condiment for these greens.

~~~~~~~~

make it easy

If you don't have Italian-seasoned broth, use two 14-ounce cans regular chicken broth and add ½ teaspoon Italian seasoning.

~~~~~~~~

1 ¼-lb. smoked turkey wing
2 16-oz. pkgs. chopped fresh collard greens
2 14-oz. cans Italian-seasoned chicken broth
5 green onions, chopped
1 green pepper, coarsely chopped
¾ t. salt
½ t. pepper
hot pepper sauce

Remove skin and meat from turkey wing, discarding skin and bone. Coarsely chop meat. Combine chopped turkey and remaining ingredients except hot pepper sauce in a slow cooker. Cover and cook on low setting for 9 hours, or until greens are tender. Serve with hot pepper sauce. Serves 10 to 12.

Scalloped Corn + Broccoli

Take this to your next potluck…your slow cooker will come back empty!

16-oz. pkg. frozen chopped broccoli
16-oz. pkg. frozen corn
10¾-oz. can cream of chicken soup
1 c. American cheese, shredded
½ c. shredded Cheddar cheese
¼ c. milk

Combine all ingredients in a large bowl and spoon into a slow cooker. Cover and cook on low setting for 5 to 6 hours. Serves 8 to 10.

Kathy Grashoff
Fort Wayne, IN

Savory Southern-Style Greens

Be sure to save the flavorful "pot liquor," or cooking broth…use it instead of water for cooking rice.

2 smoked ham hocks
6 c. water, divided
3 to 4 cubes ham bouillon
2 T. sugar
2 T. vinegar brine from a jar of sliced jalapeño peppers

seasoned salt and pepper to taste
1 bunch collard greens, trimmed and sliced into ½-inch strips
cooked rice

Combine ham hocks and 2 cups water in a stockpot; bring to a boil. Reduce heat and simmer for 15 to 30 minutes. Stir in remaining water and other ingredients except greens and rice. Transfer ham hocks and greens to a slow cooker; pour hot broth over top. Cover and cook on low setting for 8 hours or overnight, until greens are tender but not mushy, adding more water as necessary to keep slow cooker at least half full of liquid. Remove ham hocks; dice meat and return to slow cooker. For best flavor, cool and refrigerate, reheating next day at serving time. Serve over cooked rice. Serves 6 to 8.

Staci Meyers
Cocoa, FL

make it easy

When buying collard greens, select a bunch with fresh-looking leaves, making them easier to prep. Look for dark green leaves that are firm and not wilted. Avoid those showing signs of yellowing or browning.

Grandma's Corn

An old-timey potluck favorite.

8-oz. pkg. cream cheese
¼ c. butter
32-oz. pkg. frozen corn

⅓ c. sugar
Optional: 1 to 3 T. water

Let cream cheese and butter soften in slow cooker on low setting for about 10 minutes. Add corn and sugar or sugar substitute; stir well, until corn is coated with cream cheese mixture. Cover and cook on low setting for 3 to 4 hours, stirring occasionally. If corn seems too thick, add water as needed just before serving. Serves 6 to 8.

Dixie Dickson
Sachse, TX

Country Corn Pudding
Angela Lively (Baxter, TN)

With four kinds of corn, this new twist on an old favorite is scrumptious!

16-oz. pkg. frozen corn
2 11-oz. cans sweet corn & diced
    peppers
14¾-oz. can creamed corn
6½-oz. pkg. corn muffin mix

¾ c. water
¼ c. butter, melted
1 t. salt
Garnish: fresh parsley, chopped

Mix all ingredients except garnish well in a large bowl; pour into a slow cooker. Cover and cook on low setting for 5 to 6 hours, stirring after 3 hours. Garnish with fresh parsley. Serves 8.

Fettuccine Garden-Style

This can be served as a delicious, nutritious meatless meal.

1 zucchini, sliced ¼-inch thick
1 yellow squash, sliced ¼-inch thick
2 carrots, peeled and thinly sliced
1½ c. sliced mushrooms
10-oz. pkg. frozen broccoli cuts
4 green onions, sliced
1 clove garlic, minced

½ t. dried basil
½ t. pepper
¼ t. salt
1 c. grated Parmesan cheese
12-oz. pkg. fettuccine pasta, cooked
1 c. shredded mozzarella cheese
1 c. milk
2 egg yolks, beaten

Place vegetables, garlic, seasonings and Parmesan in a slow cooker. Cover and cook on high setting for 2 hours. Add remaining ingredients to slow cooker; stir to blend well. Reduce heat to low setting; cover and cook 15 to 30 more minutes. Serves 6 to 8.

Lisa Hays
Crocker, MO

Mac + Cheese

This tastes just like the old-fashioned macaroni & cheese that Grandma used to make. It is delicious and quick to prepare!

8-oz. pkg. elbow macaroni, cooked
2 eggs, beaten
12-oz. can evaporated milk
1½ c. milk
3 c. shredded sharp Cheddar cheese

½ c. margarine, melted
1 t. salt
pepper to taste
Optional: grape tomatoes, quartered

Mix together all ingredients except tomatoes, if using, in a large bowl, and pour into a lightly greased slow cooker. Cover and cook on low setting for 3 to 4 hours. Sprinkle servings with tomatoes, if desired. Serves 6 to 8.

Mary Alice Veal
Mars Hill, NC

Hot-+-Spicy Black-Eyed Peas

16-oz. pkg. dried black-eyed peas
2 c. hot water
4 green onions, chopped
1 red pepper, chopped
1 jalapeño pepper, diced
3-oz. pkg. pepperoni slices, diced

1 cube chicken bouillon
½ t. salt
¼ t. cayenne pepper
14½-oz. can Mexican-style stewed tomatoes
¾ c. quick-cooking rice, uncooked

Place peas in a large bowl. Cover with hot water 2 inches above peas; let stand 8 hours. Drain. Combine peas and remaining ingredients except tomatoes and rice in a slow cooker. Cover and cook on low setting for 8 hours, or until peas are tender. Stir in tomatoes and rice. Cover and cook for 30 more minutes, or until rice is tender. Serves 10 to 12.

Cheesy Parmesan Polenta

9 c. chicken broth
¼ c. butter, sliced
1 bay leaf

3 c. instant polenta, uncooked
3 c. grated Parmesan cheese

Bring broth, butter and bay leaf to a boil in a saucepan over medium heat. Gradually whisk in polenta; add cheese and continue whisking until well blended. Transfer to a slow cooker. Cover and cook on low setting for 25 to 30 minutes. Discard bay leaf before serving. Serves 6.

Marian Buckley
Fontana, CA

Lazy Pierogie Casserole

Serve with grilled sausages...yum!

8-oz. pkg. bowtie pasta, cooked
4 to 6 potatoes, peeled and
  sliced ½-inch thick
2 8-oz. pkgs. shredded
  Cheddar cheese

¾ c. butter, sliced
¾ c. bacon, crisply cooked and
  crumbled
1 c. onion, finely chopped
salt and pepper to taste

Layer pasta and remaining ingredients in a slow cooker. Cover and cook on low setting for 7 to 8 hours. Stir gently before serving. Serves 4 to 6.

Kelly Alderson
Erie, PA

"This creamy dish makes a great alternative to pasta or potatoes. I like to serve it topped with my favorite homemade mushroom spaghetti sauce...yum! You'll find polenta next to regular cornmeal at the grocery store."

—Marian

Cheesy Crock Potatoes

A real winner…you may want to make a double batch!

24-oz. pkg. frozen shredded
   hashbrowns, thawed
10¾-oz. can cream of potato
   soup
16-oz. container ranch dip

1 to 2 c. shredded Cheddar
   cheese
salt, pepper and garlic powder
   to taste
6-oz. can French-fried onions

Combine hashbrowns, soup, dip, cheese and seasonings in a slow cooker. Cover and cook on low setting for 4 to 6 hours, stirring once. Sprinkle with onions before serving. Serves 4 to 6.

Daphne Mann
Waukesha, WI

German Potato Salad

"I was looking for something new for Easter dinner when I ran across this recipe. I tried it and my family loved it!"

—Maureen

4 c. potatoes, peeled and cubed
6 slices bacon, crisply cooked,
   crumbled and 2 T. drippings
   reserved
¾ c. onion, chopped
10¾-oz. can cream of chicken
   soup

¼ c. water
2 T. cider vinegar
½ t. sugar
pepper and dried parsley
   to taste
Garnish: fresh parsley,
   chopped

Cover potatoes with water in a saucepan; simmer over medium heat about 15 minutes, or just until tender. Drain and let cool. Sauté onion in reserved drippings over medium-high heat until tender, about 5 minutes. Blend together soup, water, vinegar, sugar and pepper in a large bowl; add bacon and onion. Add potatoes and parsley; mix well and pour into a slow cooker. Cover and cook on low setting for 4 hours. Serve warm or at room temperature. Garnish with fresh parsley. Serves 4.

Maureen Laskovich
Allison Park, PA

German Potato Salad

Country-Style Scalloped Potatoes

Eleanor Paternoster (Bridgeport, CT)

6 russet potatoes, thinly sliced
1½ lbs. ham steak, cubed
10¾-oz. can cream of mushroom
  soup
1¼ c. water
1 c. shredded Cheddar cheese
grill seasoning to taste
Garnish: fresh chives, chopped

Layer potatoes and ham in a slow cooker that has been sprayed with non-stick vegetable spray. Combine remaining ingredients except garnish in a bowl; pour over potatoes and ham. Cover and cook on high setting for 3½ hours, or until potatoes are fork-tender. Reduce heat to low setting; continue cooking for about one hour. Garnish with chives, if desired. Serves 4 to 6.

Harvest Pecan Sweet Potatoes

2 29-oz. cans sweet potatoes, drained
⅓ c. plus 2 t. butter, melted and divided
2 T. sugar
⅓ c. plus 2 T. brown sugar, packed and divided
1 T. orange juice
2 eggs, beaten
½ c. milk
⅓ c. chopped pecans
2 T. all-purpose flour

Mash sweet potatoes in a large bowl; blend in ⅓ cup melted butter, sugar and 2 tablespoons brown sugar. Beat in orange juice, eggs and milk; spoon into a lightly greased slow cooker and set aside. Combine pecans, flour, remaining brown sugar and remaining butter in a small bowl. Spread mixture over sweet potatoes; cover and cook on high setting for 3 to 4 hours. Serves 8 to 10.

Nancy Girard
Chesapeake, VA

Smashed Redskin Potatoes

Garnish with a sprinkle of snipped fresh chives.

5 lbs. redskin potatoes, quartered
1 T. garlic, minced
3 cubes chicken bouillon
8-oz. container sour cream
8-oz. pkg. cream cheese, softened
½ c. butter, softened
salt and pepper to taste

Place potatoes, garlic and bouillon in a large saucepan; cover with water. Bring to a boil; cook just until potatoes are tender, about 15 minutes. Drain; reserve cooking liquid. Place potatoes, sour cream and cream cheese in a large bowl and mash, adding cooking liquid as needed until desired consistency is reached. Spoon into a slow cooker; cover and cook on low setting for 2 to 3 hours. Stir in butter, salt and pepper just before serving. Serves 10 to 12.

Kay Marone
Des Moines, IA

slow-cooker secrets

Fluffy mashed potatoes for a crowd will stay warm and tasty for hours...just spoon them into a slow cooker set on warm.

Louisiana Red Beans + Rice

"Sometimes we enjoy this as a meatless meal; other times I'll add a half pound of sliced smoked sausage."

—Diana

2 15-oz. cans red beans, undrained
14½-oz. can diced tomatoes, undrained
½ c. celery, chopped
½ c. green pepper, chopped

½ c. green onions, chopped
2 cloves garlic, minced
1 to 2 t. hot pepper sauce
1 t. Worcestershire sauce
1 bay leaf
cooked rice

Combine all ingredients except rice in a 4-quart slow cooker. Cover and cook on low setting for 4 to 6 hours. About 30 minutes before serving, use a potato masher to lightly mash some of the mixture until thickened. Cover again; increase heat to high setting and continue cooking for 30 minutes. Discard bay leaf. To serve, ladle over cooked rice in bowls. Serves 6.

Diana Chaney
Olathe, KS

Indian Summer Rice

Swap out the spinach for frozen broccoli, if you'd like.

1 c. onion, chopped
1 c. celery, chopped
1 c. margarine
2 10-oz. pkgs. frozen chopped spinach, thawed and drained
2 10¾-oz. cans cream of mushroom soup

3 c. instant rice, uncooked
16-oz. jar pasteurized process cheese sauce
8-oz. can sliced mushrooms, drained
½ c. warm water

Sauté onion and celery in margarine in a saucepan over medium-high heat until tender; transfer to a large bowl and stir in remaining ingredients. Mix well; spoon into a slow cooker. Cover and cook on high setting for 30 minutes. Reduce heat to low setting and cook for an additional 2 hours. Serves 8 to 10.

Kathie Williams
Oakland City, IN

Toasted Herbed Rice

3 T. butter
1¾ c. converted long-grain rice,
  uncooked
2 14-oz. cans chicken broth
¼ t. salt

6 green onions, chopped
1 t. dried basil
⅓ c. pine nuts, toasted
Garnish: fresh basil sprig

Melt butter in a large skillet over medium-high heat; add rice and sauté 4 minutes, or until golden brown. Combine sautéed rice, broth, salt, green onions and basil in a slow cooker. Cover and cook on high setting for 2 hours, or until liquid is absorbed and rice is tender. Stir in pine nuts. Garnish with basil sprig. Serves 6.

Berry Good Wild Rice

Try it…you'll never go back to plain old white rice!

1½ c. long-cooking wild rice, uncooked
2 14-oz. cans vegetable broth
4½-oz. can sliced mushrooms, drained
4 green onions, sliced
1 T. butter, melted
½ t. salt
¼ t. pepper
½ c. slivered almonds
⅓ c. sweetened dried cranberries

Mix all ingredients except almonds and cranberries in a slow cooker. Cover and cook on low setting for 4 to 5 hours, until rice is tender. About 30 minutes before serving time, place almonds in an ungreased heavy skillet over medium-low heat. Cook for 5 to 7 minutes, stirring frequently, until almonds begin to brown; stir constantly until golden and fragrant. Stir almonds and cranberries into rice mixture. Cover and cook on low setting for 15 more minutes. Serves 6.

Judith Jennings
Ironwood, MI

Spoon Bread Florentine

Deliciously different and so simple to make.

10-oz. pkg. frozen chopped
  spinach, thawed and drained
6 green onions, sliced
1 red pepper, chopped
5½-oz. pkg. cornbread mix
4 eggs, beaten
1 c. cottage cheese
½ c. butter, melted
1¼ t. seasoned salt

Combine all ingredients in a large bowl; mix well. Spoon into a lightly greased slow cooker. Cover, with lid slightly ajar to allow moisture to escape. Cook on low setting for 3 to 4 hours or on high setting for 1¾ to 2 hours, until edges are golden and a knife tip inserted in center comes out clean. Serves 8.

Jo Ann
Gooseberry Patch

slow-cooker secrets

Keep slow-cooked food hot for carry-ins…wrap the crock in several layers of newspaper and then set in an insulated cooler. Food will stay warm for up to 2 hours.

Cheddar Cheese Strata

Makes a delightful brunch dish.

8 slices bread, crusts trimmed
8-oz. pkg. shredded sharp
  Cheddar cheese
4 eggs
1 c. light cream
1 c. evaporated milk
1 T. dried parsley
¼ t. salt
Garnish: paprika, fresh parsley

Tear bread into bite-size pieces. Alternate layers of bread and cheese in a slow cooker; set aside. Whisk together eggs, cream, evaporated milk, parsley and salt in a bowl; pour over bread and cheese. Sprinkle with paprika. Cover and cook on low setting for 3 to 4 hours. Garnish with parsley. Serves 4 to 6.

Tracy McIntire
Delaware, OH

Autumn Apple-Pecan Dressing

Extra special for the holidays.

4 c. soft bread cubes	1 c. celery, chopped
1 c. saltine crackers, crushed	⅔ c. chicken broth
1½ c. apples, peeled, cored and chopped	¼ c. butter, melted
1 c. chopped pecans	2 eggs, beaten
1 c. onion, chopped	½ t. pepper
	½ t. dried sage

Combine bread cubes, cracker crumbs, apples, pecans, onion and celery in a slow cooker; set aside. Mix remaining ingredients in a small bowl until well blended. Pour into slow cooker and toss to coat. Cover and cook on low setting for 4 to 5 hours, until dressing is puffed and golden around the edges. Serves 8.

Fawn McKenzie
Wenatchee, WA

Homestyle Cornbread Dressing

Put this on the last couple of hours the turkey is baking.

8½-oz. pkg. cornbread mix
8 slices day-old bread, torn
4 eggs, beaten
1 onion, chopped
¼ c. celery, chopped
2 10¾-oz. cans cream of
  chicken soup

2 14½-oz. cans chicken broth
1½ T. dried sage
1 t. salt
¼ t. pepper
2 T. margarine, sliced

Prepare cornbread according to package directions; cool and crumble. Mix together all ingredients except margarine in a large bowl. Pour into a lightly greased slow cooker; dot with margarine. Cover and cook on low setting for 4 hours or on high setting for 2 hours. Serves 16.

Tracy Chitwood
Van Buren, MO

Holiday Sage Stuffing

1 c. butter
2 onions, chopped
4 stalks celery, chopped
¼ c. fresh parsley, chopped
12 to 13 c. day-old bread,
  cubed
1½ t. salt

1½ t. dried sage
1 t. poultry seasoning
1 t. dried thyme
½ t. pepper
3 c. vegetable or chicken
  broth
2 eggs, beaten

"This recipe is great for Thanksgiving... using the slow cooker frees up the oven for other dishes."

—Sonja

Melt butter in a skillet over medium heat. Sauté onions, celery and parsley; pour over bread cubes in a large mixing bowl. Add seasonings and toss together. Pour broth over bread and toss again; add eggs and mix. Pack lightly in a slow cooker. Cover and cook on high setting for 45 minutes. Reduce heat to low setting and cook for 4 to 6 hours. Check after 2 hours; add more broth if a moister stuffing is preferred. Serves 8 to 10.

Sonja Enright
Toms River, NJ

Eggs with Cheddar &
Bacon, page 196

all about breakfast

Start your day off right with one of these tasty recipes. Everyone will love Ham-&-Swiss Quiche and South-of-the-Border Breakfast. Try hearty Sunrise Hashbrowns or have a sweet start with Caramel-Nut Rolls. To warm up, enjoy Pumpkin Oatmeal or a cup of Mocha Cocoa. After sampling a few of these recipes, you'll agree that breakfast foods can be enjoyed any time of the day!

Eggs with Cheddar & Bacon

For a twist, try maple-flavored bacon or even pepper bacon in this recipe.

make it easy

Ham and Swiss cheese can be used in place of the bacon and Cheddar cheese if you have those on hand.

3 to 4 c. crusty bread, diced
½ lb. bacon, crisply cooked, crumbled and 1 T. drippings reserved
Optional: 2 to 3 c. favorite vegetables, chopped

8 eggs, beaten
½ c. milk
1 c. shredded Cheddar cheese
salt and pepper to taste

Place bread in a lightly greased slow cooker. If using vegetables, heat reserved drippings in a large skillet over medium heat. Sauté vegetables, tossing to coat. Stir bacon and vegetables into bread. Whisk together eggs and milk in a medium bowl; stir in cheese, salt and pepper. Pour over bread mixture. Cover and cook on low setting for 3 to 3½ hours, until eggs are set. Serves 6 to 8.

Lora Montgomery
Delaware, OH

Ranch House Breakfast

"Our family spent a week on a Texas ranch...we had a ball! And no kidding, every morning, straight from the chuck wagon, a breakfast very similar to this was served."

—Rita

3 qts. boiling water
2 T. salt
2 t. pepper
5 c. steel-cut oats, uncooked
2 lbs. ground beef

2 lbs. ground pork breakfast sausage
2 onions, finely chopped
¼ c. oil

Combine water, salt and pepper in a slow cooker. Stir in oats; cover and cook on high setting for 1½ hours. Mix together beef, pork and onions in a large bowl; stir into oat mixture. Cover and cook on low setting for 3 hours, stirring occasionally. Transfer to a 13"x9" baking pan; cool until firm. Turn out onto wax paper and chill for one hour. Cut into thin slices. Heat oil in a large, heavy skillet over medium-high heat. Fry slices until golden. Serves 20.

Rita Morgan
Pueblo, CO

Ranch House Breakfast

Ham-+-Swiss Quiche

14.1-oz. pkg. refrigerated
  pie crusts
2 c. shredded Swiss cheese,
  divided
1 c. chopped ham
4 green onions, chopped

6 eggs
1 c. whipping cream
¼ t. salt
¼ t. pepper
⅛ t. nutmeg

Cut pie crusts in half. Press 3 pie crust halves into bottom and 2 inches up sides of a greased oval slow cooker, overlapping seams by ¼ inch. Reserve remaining pie crust half for another use. Cover and cook on high setting for 1½ hours. Sprinkle one cup cheese, ham and green onions over crust. Whisk together eggs and remaining ingredients in a medium bowl; pour over ingredients in crust. Sprinkle remaining one cup cheese over egg mixture. Cover and cook on high setting for 1½ hours, or until filling is set. Uncover and let stand 5 minutes before serving. Cut quiche into wedges; serve immediately. Serves 6.

South-of-the-Border Breakfast

For a new flavor, try peach or pineapple salsa as a garnish.

1 lb. ground pork
    breakfast sausage, browned
    and drained
4-oz. can chopped green chiles
1 c. frozen peppers and
    onions, thawed and drained

2½ c. shredded Monterey Jack
    or Pepper Jack cheese
1½ doz. eggs, beaten
Garnish: sour cream, salsa

slow-cooker secrets

If you need to alter slow-cooker settings, keep this rule in mind...one hour on high is equal to two hours on low.

Layer sausage, chiles, pepper mixture and cheese in a greased slow cooker. Repeat layers until all ingredients except eggs and garnish are used, ending with a layer of cheese. Pour eggs over top. Cover and cook on low setting for 7 to 8 hours. Garnish as desired. Serves 10.

Jo Ann
Gooseberry Patch

Sunrise Hashbrowns

32-oz. pkg. frozen diced
  potatoes
2 c. cooked ham, cubed
4-oz. jar diced pimentos,
  drained

10¾-oz. can Cheddar
  cheese soup
¾ c. milk
¼ t. pepper

Combine potatoes, ham and pimentos in a slow cooker. Combine soup, milk and pepper in a bowl; pour over potato mixture. Cover and cook on low setting for 6 to 8 hours. Serves 4.

Amy Butcher
Columbus, GA

Breakie Potatoes

4 potatoes, peeled and sliced
1 T. butter, diced
1 onion, thinly sliced
4 slices bacon, crisply cooked
  and crumbled

1 c. shredded sharp
  Cheddar cheese

Layer half of each ingredient in a slow cooker in order given; repeat layering. Cover and cook on low setting for 8 to 10 hours. Serves 4.

Laura Fuller
Fort Wayne, IN

"Otherwise known as Breakfast Potatoes... our three-year-old always wants to know 'What's for breakie?'"

—Laura

Caramel-Nut Rolls

½ c. brown sugar, packed
¼ c. chopped nuts
2 8-oz. tubes refrigerated
  biscuits

¼ c. butter, melted
Garnish: cinnamon, sugar

Combine brown sugar and nuts in a small bowl. Dip each biscuit into butter and then into brown sugar mixture. Arrange biscuits in a greased 3-pound metal coffee can or a slow-cooker cake pan insert. Sprinkle each layer of biscuits lightly with cinnamon and sugar. Place can or pan in a slow cooker; if using a coffee can, cover with several layers of paper towels. Cover and cook on high setting for 3 to 4 hours. Serves 10 to 12.

Jamie Moffatt
French Lick, IN

sunrise surprise

Surprise Mom with breakfast in bed...and it doesn't have to be just on Mother's Day!

Sharon's Granola

This is a very easy and tasty recipe. Add any combination of raisins, dried fruit or nuts to suit your taste.

5 c. long-cooking oats, uncooked	½ c. honey
1 c. sweetened flaked coconut	1 t. cinnamon
½ c. oil	1 t. vanilla extract
	⅛ t. salt

Mix together all ingredients in a large bowl; place in a slow cooker sprayed with non-stick vegetable spray. Cover, leaving lid slightly ajar. Cook on low setting for 5 hours, or until golden, stirring occasionally. Serves 6.

Sharon Demers
Dolores, CO

Cinnamon-Cocoa Granola

A tasty nibble that's healthy, too!

make it easy

One of the best things about homemade granola is that there are endless combinations of cereals. Just use what you have on hand for convenience.

4 c. long-cooking oats, uncooked	⅔ c. honey
1 c. bran cereal	¼ c. oil
1 c. wheat germ	2 T. baking cocoa
½ c. sesame seed	1 t. cinnamon

Combine all ingredients in a slow cooker. Cover, leaving lid slightly ajar. Cook on low setting for about 4 hours, stirring occasionally. Cool; store in an airtight container for one to 2 weeks. Makes about 6 cups.

Melody Taynor
Everett, WA

Blueberry Breakfast Cake

Beth Kramer (Port Saint Lucie, FL)

6½-oz. pkg. blueberry muffin mix
¼ c. milk

1 egg
⅛ t. cinnamon

Reserve ¼ cup muffin mix; set aside. Spray a slow cooker with non-stick vegetable spray. Stir together remaining mix, milk, egg and cinnamon in a medium bowl just until combined; spoon into slow cooker, spreading evenly. Sprinkle with reserved mix. Cover top of slow cooker with 6 to 8 paper towels to absorb condensation. Cover; cook on high setting for one hour. Turn off slow cooker; let stand for 10 minutes. Loosen edges of cake with a knife. Place a plate on top of slow cooker; invert to remove cake. Place another plate on top of cake; invert again. Slice into wedges. Serves 6.

Grits with Gusto

If you like breakfast a little spicy...sprinkle warm grits with a tablespoon or two of shredded cheese and dollop a spoonful of hot salsa right in the middle.

2 c. long-cooking grits, uncooked
6 c. water
4-oz. can chopped green chiles
1 jalapeño pepper, seeded and finely chopped
1 t. salt
⅛ t. cayenne pepper
Optional: ½ t. paprika, ½ t. chili powder
Garnish: butter, salt and pepper

Combine all ingredients except garnish in a lightly greased slow cooker; mix well. Cover and cook on low setting for about 8 hours. Stir after first hour of cooking; stir well before serving. Serve with butter, salt and pepper. Serves 6.

Penny Sherman
Cumming, GA

Early Bird Oatmeal

You'll never have "plain" oatmeal again!

3 c. long-cooking oats,
  uncooked
¾ c. powdered sugar
¼ t. salt

21-oz. can cherry pie filling
6 c. water
1 t. almond extract

Combine oats, powdered sugar and salt in a large bowl; pour into a slow cooker that has been sprayed with non-stick vegetable spray. Add remaining ingredients; stir until combined. Cover and cook on low setting for 8 hours. Serves 4 to 6.

Lynda Robson
Boston, MA

Sweetie Banana Oatmeal

2 c. long-cooking oats,
  uncooked
½ c. sweetened
  condensed milk

4 c. water
2 bananas, thinly sliced

Combine oats, milk and water in a slow cooker that has been sprayed with non-stick vegetable spray. Cover and cook on low setting for 6 to 8 hours. Add bananas 10 to 15 minutes before serving. Serves 4.

Athena Colegrove
Big Springs, TX

"My little ones, with Daddy's help, made this for me for Valentine's Day... what a yummy breakfast from my three sweeties!"

—Athena

Berry Bog Oatmeal

Cranberries and a touch of honey turn ordinary oatmeal into breakfast the whole family looks forward to.

make it easy

Keep in mind that an equal amount of evaporated milk can be substituted if you don't have half-and-half.

1 c. steel-cut oats, uncooked
1 c. sweetened dried cranberries
1 c. chopped dates
4 c. water
½ c. half-and-half
2 T. honey

Combine oats, cranberries, dates and water in a greased slow cooker. Cover and cook on low setting for 6 to 8 hours. Stir in half-and-half and honey. Serves 4.

Elizabeth Blackstone
Racine, WI

Pumpkin Oatmeal

2 c. long-cooking oats,
  uncooked
1 c. pumpkin pie mix
2 c. milk
2 c. water

¼ c. butter
½ t. salt
Garnish: maple syrup,
  chopped nuts

Mix together all ingredients except garnish in a lightly greased slow cooker. Cover and cook on low setting for 8 hours. Serve with drizzle of maple syrup and sprinkle with nuts. Serves 6 to 8.

Shannon James
Georgetown, KY

"This is always a favorite in the fall and around the holidays. Who doesn't love waking up to the sweet and spicy aroma of pumpkin baking?"

—Shannon

Nutty Breakfast Cereal

Pour a little warm milk over individual servings…yummy!

3 c. long-cooking oats, uncooked
½ c. powdered milk
6 c. water

Optional: 1 c. chopped walnuts
1 c. creamy peanut butter
¾ c. honey
½ c. oil

Combine oats, powdered milk, water and walnuts, if using, in a slow cooker. Add remaining ingredients without mixing. Cook, uncovered, on high setting for one hour. Stir when honey and peanut butter are slightly melted. Reduce heat to low setting and continue to cook, uncovered, for 2 to 3 more hours. Serves 8 to 10.

Nola Coons
Gooseberry Patch

make it easy

Make short work of chopping nuts…seal them in a plastic zipping bag and roll with a rolling pin. No muss, no fuss!

Grammy's Porridge

Raisins and apples seem to be made for each other, and in this homestyle porridge, they taste absolutely terrific together.

¾ c. long-cooking oats, uncooked
¼ c. cracked wheat, uncooked
3 c. water
½ c. raisins

½ c. apple, peeled, cored and grated
¼ c. wheat germ
Garnish: cinnamon, milk, honey

Combine all ingredients except garnish in a slow cooker. Cover and cook on low setting for 6 to 8 hours, or overnight. Spoon into serving bowls and serve with cinnamon, milk and honey. Serves 4.

April Jacobs
Loveland, CO

Mom's Rice Porridge Samantha Sparks (Madison, WI)

You can also use medium-grain or short-grain rice in this recipe.

1 c. long-cooking rice,
  uncooked
2 c. water
12-oz. can evaporated milk

½ c. raisins
½ t. salt
Garnish: cinnamon

Combine all ingredients except garnish in a slow cooker. Cover and cook on low setting for 6 to 8 hours, or overnight. Garnish with cinnamon. Serves 2 to 4.

Snowy Day Hot Chocolate

Dana Lungerich (Frisco, TX)

14-oz. can sweetened
  condensed milk
½ c. baking cocoa
2 t. vanilla extract

6½ c. hot water
Garnish: whipped cream,
  cinnamon

Combine condensed milk, cocoa and vanilla in a slow cooker, mixing well with a whisk. Gradually stir in hot water, mixing well. Cover and cook on low setting for 3 to 4 hours, stirring occasionally. Top individual servings with whipped cream and cinnamon. Serves 8.

Viennese Coffee

This traditional recipe is very rich tasting.

3 c. strong brewed coffee
3 T. chocolate syrup
1 t. sugar
⅓ c. whipping cream
Optional: ¼ c. chocolate
   liqueur

Garnish: frozen whipped
   topping, thawed, chocolate
   shavings or curls

Combine coffee, chocolate syrup and sugar in a slow cooker. Cover and cook on low setting for 2 to 2½ hours. Stir in whipping cream and liqueur, if using. Cover and cook on low setting for 30 more minutes, or until heated through. Ladle into mugs; garnish with dollops of whipped topping and chocolate shavings or curls. Serves 4.

Robin Hill
Rochester, NY

Mocha Cocoa

Just about the best cocoa you've ever tasted!

8-oz. pkg. semi-sweet baking
   chocolate, chopped
3 c. half-and-half
2 c. milk
1 c. strong brewed coffee
2 T. brown sugar, packed
1 t. vanilla extract

1 t. cinnamon
½ t. allspice
½ t. nutmeg
⅛ t. salt
Garnish: 1 c. whipping cream,
   whipped

Combine all ingredients except whipping cream in a slow cooker; mix well. Cover and cook on high setting for one hour, or until chocolate is melted, stirring every 15 minutes. Serve immediately, or reduce heat to low setting and keep covered. Top individual mugs with a dollop of whipped cream. Serves 6.

Vickie
Gooseberry Patch

slow-cooker secrets

Fill up a slow cooker with hot chocolate before going out to enjoy snowy weather… what could be cozier when you return home?

Tropical Tea

A delightful, warming beverage for a cool day.

6 c. boiling water
6 teabags
1½ c. unsweetened
  pineapple juice
1½ c. orange juice
⅓ c. sugar
2 T. honey
1 orange, halved and sliced

Combine boiling water and teabags in a slow cooker; cover and let steep for 5 minutes. Discard teabags; stir in remaining ingredients. Cover and cook on low setting for 2 to 4 hours, until heated through. Serve in mugs or teacups. Makes about 2½ quarts.

Angela Murphy
Tempe, AZ

Herbal Apple Tea

A spiced tea the whole family can enjoy.

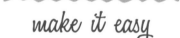

make it easy

Warm up frosty mornings with a big mug of herbal tea…just for fun, stir it with a cherry licorice whip!

3 cinnamon herbal teabags
3 c. boiling water
2 c. apple juice
6 whole cloves
4-inch cinnamon stick

Place teabags in a slow cooker. Pour boiling water over top; let stand for 10 minutes. Remove and discard teabags. Add apple juice, cloves and cinnamon stick. Cover and cook on low setting for 2 to 3 hours. Remove and discard cloves and cinnamon stick. Serves 4.

Regina Wickline
Pebble Beach, CA

Double-Delicious Cider

4 c. apple juice
12-oz. can frozen orange juice
  concentrate, thawed
½ c. water
1 T. red cinnamon candies

½ t. nutmeg
1 t. whole cloves
Optional: orange slices,
  cinnamon sticks

Combine apple juice, orange juice concentrate, water, candies and
nutmeg in a slow cooker. Place cloves in a double thickness of cheesecloth;
bring up corners of cloth and tie with kitchen string to form a bag. Add
bag to slow cooker. Cover and cook on low setting for 2 to 3 hours. Before
serving, discard spice bag and stir cider. Garnish with orange slices and
cinnamon sticks, if desired. Serves 8.

Tori Willis
Champaign, IL

Razzleberry Upside-Down
Cake, page 225

ooey-gooey desserts

Indulge your family and friends with desserts that are easy enough for weeknight suppers. Celebrate by serving a treat like Banana Pudding Cake. Hot Fudge Spoon Cake will become a family favorite. And enjoy the taste of summer, but with the convenience of frozen fruit, in Easy-Peasy Berry Cobbler.

Banana Pudding Cake

3 egg whites
1 c. bananas, mashed
18½-oz. pkg. yellow cake mix
2½ c. water, divided
3-oz. pkg. cook & serve banana pudding mix

Beat egg whites with an electric mixer at high speed until soft peaks form, about one to 2 minutes. Beat bananas in a separate bowl until puréed; add to egg whites. Add dry cake mix and ½ cup water; beat for one to 2 minutes. Set aside. Spray a slow cooker with non-stick vegetable spray. Combine remaining water and dry pudding mix in a small bowl, stirring until dissolved. Add pudding mixture to cake batter; beat for one minute or until combined. Pour cake mixture and pudding mixture into slow cooker; do not stir. Place 8 paper towels on top to absorb moisture. Cover and cook on high setting for 2 hours. Uncover slow cooker; place a large rimmed serving plate on top of slow cooker. Carefully invert cake onto plate. Serves 12.

Vickie
Gooseberry Patch

Upside-Down Blueberry Cake

Keep it simple...just spoon this cake out if you don't want to invert the slow cooker.

21-oz. can blueberry pie filling
2 eggs, separated
18¼-oz. pkg. lemon cake mix
1 c. water
⅓ c. applesauce

Spread pie filling in a slow cooker that has been sprayed with non-stick vegetable spray. Beat egg whites with an electric mixer at high speed until soft peaks form, about 2 minutes. Stir in egg yolks, cake mix, water and applesauce just until combined. Pour over filling; do not stir. Place 8 paper towels on top of slow cooker to absorb condensation. Cover and cook on high setting for 2 hours, or until a toothpick inserted near the center comes out clean. Remove crock from slow cooker; remove lid and paper towels. Cool cake for 15 minutes. Place a large serving plate over crock; carefully invert cake onto plate. Serves 10 to 12.

Missie Brown
Delaware, OH

Cranberry Upside-Down Cake

Here's a festive twist on traditional pineapple upside-down cake. Serve with ice cream or sweetened whipped cream to complement the tart cranberries.

1 c. light brown sugar, packed
½ c. butter, melted
14-oz. can whole-berry
  cranberry sauce
12-oz. pkg. fresh cranberries

16-oz. pkg. pound cake mix
¾ c. milk
2 eggs
½ t. almond extract

Stir together brown sugar, butter and cranberry sauce in a small bowl until blended. Pour mixture into a lightly greased slow cooker. Top with cranberries. Beat pound cake mix, milk, eggs and almond extract with an electric mixer at low speed 30 seconds, scraping bowl constantly. Beat at low speed for 2 more minutes. Pour batter over cranberries. Cover and cook on high setting for 2 hours and 10 minutes, or until a toothpick inserted in the center comes out clean. Turn off slow cooker; let cake stand, covered, 20 minutes. Invert cake onto a serving platter. Serves 8 to 10.

Hot Fudge Spoon Cake

Heavenly!

1 c. all-purpose flour
1¾ c. light brown sugar,
   packed and divided
¼ c. plus 3 T. baking cocoa,
   divided
2 t. baking powder

¼ t. salt
½ c. milk
2 T. butter, melted
½ t. vanilla extract
1¾ c. hot water
Garnish: vanilla ice cream

Combine flour, one cup brown sugar, 3 tablespoons cocoa, baking powder and salt in a medium bowl. Whisk in milk, melted butter and vanilla. Spread evenly in a slow cooker. Mix together remaining brown sugar and cocoa in a small bowl; sprinkle evenly over top of batter. Pour in hot water; do not stir. Cover and cook on high setting for 2 hours, or until a toothpick inserted one inch deep comes out clean. Spoon warm cake into bowls; top with vanilla ice cream. Serves 6.

Sara Plott
Monument, CO

slow-cooker secrets

If it's time to buy a new slow cooker, look for one with a removable crock...they're so much easier to clean!

Chocolate-Peanut Butter Cake

18½-oz. pkg. chocolate cake
   mix, divided
⅓ c. creamy peanut butter

½ c. chopped nuts
½ c. water

Measure 2 cups cake mix into a large bowl; reserve remaining mix for another recipe. Add remaining ingredients to bowl; mix well. Beat by hand for about 2 minutes. Pour into a greased and floured 2-pound metal coffee can. Place can in a slow cooker; cover top of can with 8 paper towels to absorb condensation. Cover and cook on high setting for 2 to 3 hours. Cool for 5 minutes. Slide a knife around edge of can and carefully turn out cake onto a serving plate. Serves 10 to 12.

Rogene Rogers
Bemidji, MN

"This cake is made in a coffee can. When it's done, I take it out of the coffee can, slice it and drizzle servings with a little hot fudge sauce. This is a sure-fire cure for chocolate and peanut butter cravings."

—Rogene

Triple Chocolate Cake
Joan Brochu (Hardwick, VT)

You can also add some raspberries on top of the ice cream.

15.25-oz. pkg. chocolate cake mix
12-oz. pkg. chocolate chips
8-oz. container sour cream
3.9-oz. pkg. instant chocolate
   pudding mix

4 eggs, beaten
1 c. water
¾ c. oil
Optional: vanilla ice cream

Place all ingredients except ice cream in a slow cooker; mix well. Cover and cook on high setting for 3 to 4 hours. If desired, serve with ice cream. Serves 8 to 10.

Cinnamon
Streusel Cake

Cinnamon Streusel Cake

A delightful brunch treat, too.

16-oz. pkg. pound cake mix
¼ c. brown sugar, packed
1 T. all-purpose flour
1 t. cinnamon
¼ c. nuts, finely chopped
Garnish: ice cream

Prepare cake mix batter according to package directions. Pour into a generously greased and floured 2-pound metal coffee can. Mix brown sugar, flour, cinnamon and nuts in a small bowl; sprinkle over batter. Cover can with 6 to 8 paper towels to absorb condensation; place in a slow cooker. Cover and cook on high setting for 3 to 4 hours. Serve with a scoop of ice cream. Serves 10.

Sharon Jones
Oklahoma City, OK

Fudgy Pudding Cake

18½-oz. pkg. chocolate cake mix
3.9-oz. pkg. instant chocolate pudding mix
16-oz. container sour cream
¾ c. oil
4 eggs
1 c. water
6-oz. pkg. semi-sweet chocolate chips
Garnish: vanilla ice cream

Mix together all ingredients except ice cream in a large bowl. Pour into a slow cooker that has been sprayed with non-stick vegetable spray. Cover and cook on low setting for 6 to 8 hours. Turn off slow cooker and let stand 20 to 30 minutes; do not lift lid until ready to serve. Serve with vanilla ice cream. Serves 8 to 10.

Carol McMillion
Catawba, VA

"This is scrump-delicious! A friend brought it to the last two covered-dish dinners at our church...it disappeared very quickly!"

—Carol

Lemon-Poppy Seed Cake

An upside-down cake that makes its own custard-like topping...yum!

15.8-oz. lemon-poppy seed
  bread mix
1 egg, beaten
8-oz. container sour cream

1¼ c. water, divided
1 T. butter
½ c. sugar
¼ c. lemon juice

Combine bread mix, egg, sour cream and ½ cup water in a mixing bowl. Stir until well moistened; spread in a lightly greased slow cooker. Combine remaining water, butter, sugar and lemon juice in a small saucepan; bring to a boil. Pour boiling mixture over batter in slow cooker; cover and cook on high setting for 2 to 2½ hours. Edges will be golden. Turn off slow cooker; let cake cool in slow cooker for about 30 minutes with lid ajar. When cool enough to handle, hold a large plate over top of slow cooker and invert to turn out cake. Serves 10 to 12.

Rogene Rogers
Bemidji, MN

Berry Patch Shortcake

"We have a pick-your-own berry patch just down the road from our home...one Saturday we took the kids and had a grand time!"

—Cathy

2¼ c. pancake mix
¾ c. sugar, divided
⅔ c. milk
3 T. applesauce

1 qt. strawberries, hulled
  and sliced
Garnish: frozen whipped
  topping, thawed

Combine pancake mix, ½ cup sugar, milk and applesauce in a bowl; stir until a dough forms. Spray a slow cooker with non-stick vegetable spray. Pat dough into bottom of slow cooker. Cover and cook on high setting for one hour and 15 minutes, or until a toothpick inserted in the center comes out clean. Toss together strawberries and remaining sugar in a bowl. Turn shortcake out of slow cooker onto a plate; slice into wedges and split. Spoon berries over top; dollop with whipped topping. Serves 8.

Cathy Hillier
Salt Lake City, UT

Lemon-Poppy Seed Cake

Peachy Dump Cake

Equally scrumptious with cherry or apple pie filling...try any favorite flavor. You can't miss!

2 14½-oz. cans peach pie
   filling
1 t. lemon juice
18½-oz. pkg. yellow cake mix
½ c. chopped pecans

½ c. butter, melted
Garnish: frozen whipped
   topping, thawed, or vanilla
   ice cream, mint sprigs

Pour pie filling into a slow cooker that has been sprayed with non-stick vegetable spray. Drizzle with lemon juice. Combine dry cake mix, pecans and melted butter in a bowl. Spread over pie filling. Cover and cook on low setting for 4 hours or on high setting for 2 hours. Serve with whipped topping or ice cream, and garnish with mint sprigs. Serves 6 to 8.

Autry Dotson
Sedalia, MO

Razzleberry Upside-Down Cake

The name may make you giggle, but this cake is so delicious that it will soon be a family favorite. You can just spoon it right out of the slow cooker.

3 **egg whites**
1¼ c. **water**
⅓ c. **applesauce**
0.3-oz. pkg. **sugar-free raspberry gelatin mix**
18¼-oz. pkg. **cherry chip cake mix**

12-oz. can **red raspberry pastry filling**
Garnish: **fresh raspberries; frozen whipped topping, thawed**

Beat egg whites in a large bowl with an electric mixer at high speed for one to 2 minutes, until soft peaks form. Add water, applesauce, gelatin mix and cake mix; beat at medium speed for 2 minutes. Spread raspberry filling into a slow cooker that has been sprayed with non-stick vegetable spray; pour cake batter mixture over top. Do not stir. Cover with 8 paper towels. Cover and cook on high setting for 2 hours. Remove crock from slow cooker; let cool for 15 minutes. Place a large rimmed serving plate on top of slow cooker. Carefully invert cake onto plate. Garnish with fresh raspberries and a dollop of whipped topping. Serves 10 to 12.

Donna Fisher
Delaware, OH

slow-cooker secrets

Keep the slow-cooker insert sparkling clean! To remove cooked-on stains, make a paste of equal parts of cream of tartar and vinegar. Just rub it on and then rinse well.

more flavor options

You can use other fruit pastry fillings in Razzleberry Upside-Down Cake. Options include mixed berry, blueberry, cherry or strawberry pastry fillings. You can also use other gelatin and cake flavors. The recipe options are limited only by your imagination. Be creative and try your favorite flavors!

Hot Fudge
Brownies

Hot Fudge Brownies

20-oz. pkg. brownie mix
1 c. chocolate syrup
1 c. hot water

Optional: vanilla ice cream or
frozen whipped topping,
thawed, maraschino
cherries, sprinkles

Prepare brownies according to package instructions, except for baking. Spray a slow cooker with non-stick vegetable spray. Spread brownie batter evenly into slow cooker. Mix together syrup and hot water in a bowl; pour evenly over brownie mixture. Cover and cook on high setting for 2½ to 3 hours, until edges are set. Remove lid; let stand for 30 minutes, or until set. Spoon onto serving plates. Serve with ice cream or whipped topping, if desired. Garnish with cherries and sprinkles, if desired. Serves 8.

Jewel Sharpe
Raleigh, NC

"This is a favorite recipe I make for camping trips...a chocolatey dessert everyone loves."

—Jewel

Raspberry Brownies in a Jar

2 1-pt. wide-mouth canning
   jars and lids, sterilized
½ c. butter, sliced
2 1-oz. sqs. unsweetened
   baking chocolate, chopped
2 eggs, beaten

¾ c. sugar
⅓ c. seedless raspberry jam
1 t. vanilla extract
¾ c. all-purpose flour
¼ t. baking powder
1 c. water

Grease and flour canning jars; set aside. Melt butter and chocolate together in a medium saucepan over low heat. Remove from heat; stir in eggs, sugar, jam and vanilla. Beat lightly with a spoon until combined. Stir in flour and baking powder; pour into prepared jars. Cover jars tightly with greased aluminum foil, greased-side down. Place jars in a slow cooker; pour one cup water around jars. Cover and cook on high setting for 3 to 3½ hours, until a toothpick inserted in the center comes out clean. Remove jars from slow cooker; cool for 10 minutes. Use a metal spatula to loosen brownies; turn out of jars. Cool brownies completely on a wire rack before slicing. Serves 12.

Laurie Wilson
Fort Wayne, IN

"It's fun to give these brownies in their jars as gifts...my family just loves them!"

—Laurie

Tropical Cobbler
Cheri Maxwell (Gulf Breeze, FL)

Pineapple brings a refreshing flavor to homestyle cobbler.

18½-oz. pkg. yellow cake mix,
   divided
20-oz. can crushed pineapple,
   undrained and divided

Garnish: frozen whipped topping,
   thawed, fresh pineapple wedges,
   toasted coconut

Set aside ⅓ cup dry cake mix. Spray a slow cooker with non-stick vegetable spray; sprinkle half of remaining dry cake mix in slow cooker. Spread half the crushed pineapple with juice over cake mix. Repeat layering. Sprinkle reserved cake mix over final layer of pineapple. Cover and cook on high setting for 2 hours. Serve with whipped topping, pineapple wedges and coconut. Serves 6 to 8.

Mom's Blueberry Cobbler

2 8-oz. tubes refrigerated
   biscuits, separated and
   quartered
⅓ c. brown sugar, packed

½ t. cinnamon
⅓ c. butter, melted
21-oz. can blueberry pie
   filling, divided

Spray a slow cooker with non-stick vegetable spray and layer one package of biscuits inside. Mix together brown sugar, cinnamon and melted butter in a small bowl just until combined; sprinkle half the mixture over biscuit layer. Spread half the pie filling over top. Layer in remaining biscuits; sprinkle with remaining brown sugar mixture and top with remaining pie filling. Cover and cook on high setting for 2½ to 3 hours, until biscuits are golden. Serves 6 to 8.

Sharon Tillman
Hampton, VA

"Growing up, I always loved blueberries...I still do! Mom would make this easy recipe that uses pie filling so I could have her yummy cobbler any time of year."

—Sharon

Easy-Peasy Berry Cobbler

Tastes like summer...couldn't be simpler to make!

16-oz. pkg. frozen mixed
   berries
½ c. sugar
12-oz. tube refrigerated
   biscuits

cinnamon to taste
Optional: vanilla ice cream

Pour frozen berries into a slow cooker and stir in sugar. Arrange biscuits on top; sprinkle with cinnamon to taste. Cover and cook on high setting for 3 hours. Serve warm with vanilla ice cream, if desired. Serves 8 to 12.

Jessica Zelkovich
Greenfield, IN

Golden Peach Cobbler

This is also yummy served with a dollop of whipping cream.

⅓ c. biscuit baking mix
⅔ c. quick-cooking oats,
   uncooked
½ c. brown sugar, packed

1 t. cinnamon
4 c. sliced peaches
½ c. peach juice or water
Optional: vanilla ice cream

Combine baking mix, oats, brown sugar and cinnamon in a slow cooker. Stir in peaches and juice or water. Cover and cook on low setting for 5 to 6 hours. If desired, remove lid for last 30 minutes to crisp the top. Serve with ice cream, if desired. Serves 4 to 6.

Jennifer Vallimont
Kersey, PA

Double-Berry Cobbler

1 c. all-purpose flour
1½ c. sugar, divided
1 t. baking powder
¼ t. salt
¼ t. cinnamon
¼ t. nutmeg
2 eggs, beaten
2 T. milk

2 T. oil
2 c. blackberries
2 c. blueberries
¾ c. water
1 t. orange zest
Optional: vanilla ice cream or
    frozen whipped topping,
    thawed

Combine flour, ¾ cup sugar, baking powder, salt and spices in a medium bowl; set aside. Combine eggs, milk and oil in a small bowl; stir into flour mixture until moistened. Spread batter evenly in a slow cooker; set aside. Combine berries, water, zest and remaining sugar in a large saucepan. Bring to a boil; remove from heat and pour over batter without stirring. Cover and cook on high setting for 2 to 2½ hours, until a toothpick inserted in the center comes out clean. Uncover and let stand 30 minutes. Spoon into bowls, topped with ice cream or whipped topping, if desired. Serves 6.

Becky Weatherman
Mocksville, NC

make it faster

Stock up during berry-picking season for delicious desserts! Lay unwashed berries on baking sheets and freeze; then pack into bags for the freezer. When you're ready to use them, rinse berries in a colander. They'll thaw quickly.

Apple Pie

Serve with ice cream or a pitcher of fresh cream for drizzling...yummy!

8 Granny Smith apples,
  peeled, cored and sliced
1¼ t. cinnamon
¼ t. allspice
¼ t. nutmeg
1½ c. biscuit baking mix,
  divided

¾ c. milk
2 T. butter, softened
¾ c. sugar
2 eggs, beaten
2 t. vanilla extract
⅓ c. brown sugar, packed
3 T. butter, chilled

Toss apple slices with spices in a large bowl; place in a lightly greased slow cooker. Combine ½ cup baking mix, milk, softened butter, sugar, eggs and vanilla in a bowl; spoon over apples. Combine remaining baking mix with brown sugar in a bowl; cut in cold butter until crumbly. Sprinkle over apple mixture. Cover and cook on low setting for 6 to 7 hours, until apples are tender. Serves 6.

Mandy Bridges
Tunnel Hill, GA

Southern Caramel Pie

"Here in Nashville, one of the country clubs always served the most delicious caramel pie made with sweetened condensed milk. This recipe is an easy way to make one in the slow cooker."

—Judy

2 14-oz. cans sweetened
  condensed milk
9-inch graham cracker crust
Garnish: frozen whipped
  topping, thawed

Optional: mini semi-sweet
  chocolate chips

Pour condensed milk into a slow cooker that has been sprayed with non-stick vegetable spray. Cover and cook on low setting for 3½ to 4 hours, stirring every 15 minutes after 2½ hours. Spoon into crust (the mixture should be golden and should be spooned in before it gets too thick). Chill well. Top with whipped topping and chocolate chips, if desired. Cooking times could vary depending on the size of your slow cooker. Mixture will appear lumpy but will thin with stirring. Serves 6 to 8.

Judy Collins
Nashville, TN

Apple Pie

Cozy Apple Bread Pudding

Sprinkle with a dash of cinnamon.

8 to 9 slices cinnamon-raisin
   bread, cubed
3 eggs, beaten
2 c. milk

½ c. sugar
21-oz. can apple pie filling
Optional: whipped cream or
   vanilla ice cream

Spread bread cubes in a single layer on an ungreased baking sheet. Bake at 300 degrees for 10 to 15 minutes, until dry, stirring twice. Cool. Whisk together eggs, milk and sugar in a large bowl. Gently stir in pie filling and bread cubes. Pour into a slow cooker that has been sprayed with non-stick vegetable spray. Cover and cook on low setting for 3 hours, or until puffy and a knife inserted near the center comes out clean. Uncover and let stand for 30 to 45 minutes; pudding will fall as it cools. Spoon into dessert dishes; garnish as desired. Serves 6.

Roseann Floura
Rockwall, TX

Country-Style Bread Pudding

¾ c. brown sugar, packed
6 slices cinnamon-raisin
  bread, buttered and cubed

4 eggs, beaten
1 qt. milk
1½ t. vanilla extract

Sprinkle brown sugar in a slow cooker that has been sprayed with non-stick vegetable spray. Add cubed bread without stirring. Beat together eggs, milk and vanilla in a large bowl; pour over bread. Cover and cook on high setting for 2 to 3 hours, until thickened. Do not stir. Spoon pudding into individual serving dishes and drizzle brown sugar sauce from slow cooker over pudding. Serves 8 to 10.

Patricia Wissler
Harrisburg, PA

"This is the best-tasting bread pudding, and it's so much easier than making it in the oven." It's delicious sprinkled with powdered sugar.

—Patricia

Steamed Cranberry Pudding

2 T. butter, softened
2 T. sugar
1⅓ c. all-purpose flour
1 t. baking powder
1 t. baking soda
½ t. salt
2 c. cranberries, halved
½ c. molasses
⅓ c. hot water

Butter a one-pound metal coffee can or pudding mold that will fit into your slow cooker; sprinkle with sugar and set aside. Combine flour, baking powder, baking soda and salt in a mixing bowl; stir in berries. Add molasses and hot water; mix well and pour into prepared can or mold. Place 2 paper towels on top of can to absorb condensation; cover tightly with aluminum foil. Set can in slow cooker; pour about 2 inches of water around can. Cover and cook on high setting for 5 to 6 hours. Let cool 10 minutes; turn pudding out of can. Slice and serve with Butter Sauce. Serves 8.

Butter Sauce:

1 c. sugar
½ c. butter
½ c. light cream
1 t. vanilla extract

Bring all ingredients to a boil in a medium saucepan; reduce heat and cook for 4 minutes. Serve warm.

Janet Girouard
Jaffrey, NH

just-desserts party

For an affordable casual get-together, invite friends over for "just desserts"! Offer two or three simple home-baked desserts such as Steamed Cranberry Pudding, a fruit pie, ice cream and a steamy pot of coffee…they'll love it.

Rogene's Homestyle Custard

2 c. milk
5 eggs, beaten
⅓ c. super-fine sugar
1 t. vanilla extract
⅛ t. salt
¼ t. nutmeg
Garnish: frozen whipped
    topping, thawed

Mix together all ingredients except nutmeg and whipped topping in a large bowl; pour into a slow cooker. Sprinkle nutmeg over top. Cover and cook on low setting for 8 hours. Serve with whipped topping, if desired. Serves 4 to 6.

Rogene Rogers
Bemidji, MN

"We love old-fashioned baked custard and enjoy this version made in the slow cooker. If you like, add ¼ cup sweetened flaked coconut."

—Rogene

Pumpkin Pie
Pudding

Pumpkin Pie Pudding

Almost as good as Grandma's…practically bakes itself!

15-oz. can pumpkin
12-oz. can evaporated milk
¾ c. sugar
½ c. biscuit baking mix
2 eggs, beaten

2 T. butter, melted
2½ t. pumpkin pie spice
Optional: frozen whipped
   topping, thawed, nutmeg

Mix together all ingredients except whipped topping and nutmeg in a bowl; pour into a greased slow cooker. Cover and cook on low setting for 6 to 7 hours. Serve with whipped topping and sprinkle with nutmeg, if desired. Serves 8.

Rhonda Reeder
Ellicott City, MD

make it easy

To save clean-up time, use cold water, not hot, to wash bowls eggs were beaten in… surprisingly, hot water makes the egg tougher to remove.

Creamy Rice Pudding

A tummy-warming treat!

1 pt. half-and-half
3 eggs
⅔ c. sugar
2 t. vanilla extract

1½ c. cooked rice
¾ c. raisins
½ t. nutmeg
½ t. cinnamon

Beat half-and-half, eggs, sugar and vanilla in a mixing bowl with an electric mixer at medium speed. Stir in rice and raisins. Pour into a greased slow cooker; sprinkle with nutmeg and cinnamon. Cover and cook on high setting for 30 minutes; stir well. Reduce heat to low setting; cover and cook for 2 to 3 hours. Serves 8 to 10.

Shelley Sparks
Amarillo, TX

Tapioca Pudding

"My husband is very fond of tapioca pudding, so I was delighted to find this recipe for the slow cooker."

—Betty

2 qts. milk
1 c. pearled tapioca, uncooked
1 to 1½ c. sugar
4 eggs, beaten

1 t. vanilla extract
Garnish: whipped cream, sliced fruit

Combine milk, tapioca and sugar in a slow cooker; stir to mix. Cover and cook on high setting for 3 hours. Whisk together eggs and vanilla in a large bowl; gradually add hot milk mixture. Pour back into slow cooker. Cover and cook on high setting for 20 more minutes. Chill until ready to serve; garnish as desired. Serves 10 to 12.

Betty Kozlowski
Newnan, GA

Sweet Cherry Flan

5 eggs, beaten
½ c. sugar
½ t. salt
¾ c. all-purpose flour
12-oz. can evaporated milk

1 t. vanilla extract
16-oz. pkg. frozen dark sweet
   cherries, thawed and drained
Garnish: powdered sugar

Beat eggs, sugar and salt in a large bowl with an electric mixer at high speed until mixture is thick and yellow. Add flour; beat until smooth. Add evaporated milk and vanilla; beat well. Pour batter into a well-greased slow cooker. Arrange cherries evenly over batter. Cover and cook on low setting for 3½ to 4 hours, until flan is firm. Garnish individual servings with powdered sugar. Serves 6.

"When I prepare this easy slow-cooker flan, I dollop servings with homemade whipped cream and lightly dust with cinnamon."

—Mary

Mary Murray
Mt. Vernon, OH

Apple-Cranberry Dessert

6 apples, peeled, cored
  and sliced
1 c. cranberries
1 c. sugar
½ t. orange zest

½ c. water
3 T. port wine or orange juice
Optional: whipping cream,
  orange zest

Arrange apples and cranberries in a lightly greased slow cooker; sprinkle with sugar. Add orange zest, water and wine or juice. Stir to mix. Cover and cook on low setting for 4 to 6 hours, until apples are tender. Spoon into serving bowls; pour whipping cream over top and garnish with orange zest, if desired. Serves 6.

Megan Brooks
Antioch, TN

Favorite Caramel Apples

Press candy-coated chocolates, candy corn, red cinnamon candies or chocolate chips into the warm caramel for a special treat.

2 14-oz. pkgs. caramels,
  unwrapped
¼ c. water
½ t. cinnamon

8 wooden skewers
8 apples
Optional: chopped nuts

Combine caramels, water and cinnamon in a slow cooker. Cover and cook on high setting for one to 1½ hours, stirring frequently. Insert sticks into apples. Reduce heat to low setting. Dip apples into hot caramel and turn to coat, scraping excess caramel from bottom of apples. Roll in chopped nuts, if desired. Place on greased wax paper to cool. Makes 8.

Graceann Frederico
Irondequoit, NY

make it easy

Make caramel apples extra special! Place semi-sweet chocolate chips in a plastic zipping bag. Microwave briefly on high until chocolate melts and then snip off a small corner of bag and drizzle melted chocolate over apples.

Favorite Caramel
Apples

Bananas Foster

Guests will flip over this decadent dessert!

½ c. butter, melted
¼ c. brown sugar, packed
6 bananas, cut into 1-inch
   slices

¼ c. rum or ¼ t. rum extract
vanilla ice cream

Stir together butter, brown sugar, bananas and rum or extract in a slow cooker. Cover and cook on low setting for one hour. To serve, spoon over scoops of ice cream. Serves 4.

Jo Ann
Gooseberry Patch

Caramel-Rum Fondue

Makes a scrumptious ending to a slow-cooker appetizer party.

make it easy

Core apples and pears in a jiffy...cut the fruit in half and then use a melon baller to scoop out the center.

25 caramels, unwrapped
⅓ c. whipping cream
¼ c. mini marshmallows

2 t. rum or ¼ t. rum extract
apple wedges, pound cake
   squares

Combine caramels and whipping cream in a slow cooker. Cover and cook on low setting 30 minutes to one hour, until melted. Stir in marshmallows and rum or extract. Cover and cook 30 more minutes. Serve with apple wedges or cake squares for dipping. Serves 6 to 8.

Ellie Brandel
Clackamas, OR

Caramel-Rum
Fondue

Banana Bread

A small loaf pan can be used if your slow cooker is oval.

⅓ c. shortening
½ c. sugar
2 eggs
1¾ c. all-purpose flour
1 t. baking powder

½ t. baking soda
½ t. salt
1 c. bananas, mashed
½ c. raisins

Blend together shortening and sugar in a mixing bowl; add eggs and beat well. Combine flour, baking powder, baking soda and salt in a separate bowl. Add dry ingredients alternately with bananas; stir in raisins. Pour batter into a greased 4-cup metal coffee can. Cover top of can with 6 to 8 paper towels to absorb condensation; set on a rack in a slow cooker. Cover and cook on high setting for 2 to 3 hours, until bread is done. Let cool slightly; turn out of can to finish cooling. Makes one loaf.

Ellie Brandel
Clackamas, OR

Zucchini-Walnut Bread

With this tasty recipe, there's no such thing as too many zucchini!

2 eggs
⅔ c. oil
1¼ c. sugar
2 t. vanilla extract
1⅓ c. zucchini, peeled and
  shredded

2 c. all-purpose flour
1 t. cinnamon
½ t. baking powder
½ t. nutmeg
¼ t. salt
½ to 1 c. chopped walnuts

Beat eggs until light and foamy in a mixing bowl with an electric mixer at high speed. Add oil, sugar, vanilla and zucchini; mix well and set aside. Mix remaining ingredients in another bowl; add to egg mixture and mix well. Pour into a greased and floured 2-pound metal coffee can or a 2-quart mold. Cover top with 8 paper towels to absorb condensation; set in a slow cooker. Cover and cook on high setting for 3 to 4 hours. Let stand 5 minutes before unmolding. Makes one loaf.

Lisa Ragland
Columbus, OH

slow-cooker secrets

Don't worry about slow-cooking temperatures being below what's considered safe for cooking. The low setting is about 200 degrees, while the high setting is about 300 degrees…both well above the safe temperature of 140 degrees.

bake ahead

Most breads can be baked and then frozen up to four months…what a time-saver! Cool completely after baking and then wrap well in plastic wrap and two layers of aluminum foil before freezing. To serve, thaw overnight in the refrigerator, bring to room temperature and warm slightly in the microwave.

Triple Chocolate-Covered Peanut Clusters

make it faster

Make these ahead for your next party or for gift-giving. Clusters may be frozen up to one month.

16-oz. jar dry-roasted peanuts

16-oz. jar unsalted dry-roasted peanuts

18 2-oz. sqs. melting chocolate, cut in half

12-oz. pkg. semi-sweet chocolate chips

4-oz. pkg. German chocolate baking squares, broken into pieces

9.75-oz. can salted whole cashews

1 t. vanilla extract

Combine all ingredients except cashews and vanilla in a slow cooker. Cover and cook on low setting for 2 hours, or until melted. Stir chocolate mixture. Add cashews and vanilla, stirring well to coat cashews. Drop nut mixture by heaping tablespoonfuls onto wax paper. Let stand until firm. Store in an airtight container. Makes 5 pounds, or about 60 clusters.

A Bunch of Crunch Candy

2 lbs. white melting chocolate,
  broken into small pieces
1½ c. creamy peanut butter
Optional: ½ t. almond
  extract

4 c. corn & oat cereal
4 c. crispy rice cereal
4 c. mini marshmallows

Place chocolate in a slow cooker. Cover and cook on high setting for one hour. Add peanut butter; stir in extract, if desired. Combine cereals and marshmallows in a large bowl. Stir into chocolate mixture until well coated. Drop by tablespoonfuls onto wax paper; let stand until set. Store, covered, at room temperature. Makes about 6½ dozen.

Marlene Darnell
Newport Beach, CA

Nutty Chocolate Fudge

3 8-oz. pkgs. dark melting
  chocolate
4 6-oz. pkgs. white melting
  chocolate
4-oz. pkg. sweet baking
  chocolate, chopped

12-oz. pkg. semi-sweet
  chocolate chips
2 12-oz. jars salted peanuts

"My mom swears this is the best fudge she has ever tasted!"

—Patricia

Place dark chocolate, white chocolate and sweet chocolate in a slow cooker; cover and cook on low setting for 2 hours, or until melted. Add chocolate chips and peanuts; continue to cook, covered, on low setting. Stir; cover and cook for one more hour. Stir again and cook for one more hour. Drop by tablespoonfuls onto wax paper; cool completely. Store in an airtight container for up to 3 months. Makes about 4 dozen pieces.

Patricia Barnett
Hillsboro, MO

METRIC EQUIVALENTS

The recipes that appear in this cookbook use the standard U.S. method for measuring liquid and dry or solid ingredients (teaspoons, tablespoons and cups). The information in the following charts is provided to help cooks outside the United States successfully use these recipes. All equivalents are approximate.

METRIC EQUIVALENTS FOR DIFFERENT TYPES OF INGREDIENTS

A standard cup measure of a dry or solid ingredient will vary in weight depending on the type of ingredient.
A standard cup of liquid is the same volume for any type of liquid.
Use the following chart when converting standard cup measures to grams (weight) or milliliters (volume).

Standard Cup	Fine Powder (ex. flour)	Grain (ex. rice)	Granular (ex. sugar)	Liquid Solids (ex. butter)	Liquid (ex. milk)
1	140 g	150 g	190 g	200 g	240 ml
¾	105 g	113 g	143 g	150 g	180 ml
⅔	93 g	100 g	125 g	133 g	160 ml
½	70 g	75 g	95 g	100 g	120 ml
⅓	47 g	50 g	63 g	67 g	80 ml
¼	35 g	38 g	48 g	50 g	60 ml
⅛	18 g	19 g	24 g	25 g	30 ml

USEFUL EQUIVALENTS FOR LIQUID INGREDIENTS BY VOLUME

¼ tsp	=							1 ml
½ tsp	=							2 ml
1 tsp	=							5 ml
3 tsp	=	1 Tbsp			=	½ fl oz	=	15 ml
		2 Tbsp	=	⅛ c	=	1 fl oz	=	30 ml
		4 Tbsp	=	¼ c	=	2 fl oz	=	60 ml
		5⅓ Tbsp	=	⅓ c	=	3 fl oz	=	80 ml
		8 Tbsp	=	½ c	=	4 fl oz	=	120 ml
		10⅔ Tbsp	=	⅔ c	=	5 fl oz	=	160 ml
		12 Tbsp	=	¾ c	=	6 fl oz	=	180 ml
		16 Tbsp	=	1 c	=	8 fl oz	=	240 ml
		1 pt	=	2 c	=	16 fl oz	=	480 ml
		1 qt	=	4 c	=	32 fl oz	=	960 ml
						33 fl oz	=	1000 ml = 1 liter

USEFUL EQUIVALENTS FOR DRY INGREDIENTS BY WEIGHT

(To convert ounces to grams, multiply the number of ounces by 30.)

1 oz	=	1/16 lb	=	30 g
4 oz	=	¼ lb	=	120 g
8 oz	=	½ lb	=	240 g
12 oz	=	¾ lb	=	360 g
16 oz	=	1 lb	=	480 g

USEFUL EQUIVALENTS FOR LENGTH

(To convert inches to centimeters, multiply the number of inches by 2.5.)

1 in			=	2.5 cm		
6 in	=	½ ft	=	15 cm		
12 in	=	1 ft	=	30 cm		
36 in	=	3 ft	= 1 yd	=	90 cm		
40 in			=	100 cm	=	1 meter

USEFUL EQUIVALENTS FOR COOKING/OVEN TEMPERATURES

	Fahrenheit	Celsius	Gas Mark
Freeze Water	32° F	0° C	
Room Temperature	68° F	20° C	
Boil Water	212° F	100° C	
Bake	325° F	160° C	3
	350° F	180° C	4
	375° F	190° C	5
	400° F	200° C	6
	425° F	220° C	7
	450° F	230° C	8
Broil			Grill

index

mains

sandwiches

sides